Billie Eilish

Your Power

The Illustrated Biography

Carolyn McHugh

sona BOOKS

sona BOOKS

© Danann Media Publishing Limited 2025

First published in the UK 2022 by Sona Books an imprint of Danann Media Publishing Ltd.

WARNING: For private domestic use only, any unauthorised copying, hiring, lending or public performance of this book is illegal.

CAT NO: SON0521

Photography courtesy of

Getty images:

- Kevin Mazur
- Jeff Kravitz/FilmMagic
- Mick Hutson/Redferns
- Lester Cohen
- Frank Hoensch/Redferns
- Medios y Media
- Stefanie Keenan
- Araya Doheny/WireImage
- Craig Barritt
- FilmMagic
- Jim Spellman/FilmMagic
- Lorne Thomson/Redferns
- Frederic J.Brown / AFP
- Tim Mosenfelder
- Michael Hickey
- Jim Bennett
- Steve Granitz/WireImage
- Rich Fury
- Frazer Harrison
- Mike Marsland/WireImage
- Tolga Akmen / AFP
- Robyn Beck / AFP
- Kevin Winter
- Mike Kemp/In Pictures
- Kevin Mazur/MG21
- Cindy Ord/MG22
- Matt Winkelmeyer
- David Cliff/NurPhoto
- Jeremychanphotography
- Suzanne Cordeiro / AFP

Alamy images:

- Sipa US
- Pacific Press Media Production Corp
- Gonzales Photo
- Christian Bertrand

- Grunge illustration designed by kjpargeter / Freepik

Book layout & design © Danann Media Publishing Limited 2022
Copy Editor Juliette O'Neill

All rights reserved. No Part of this title may be reproduced or transmitted in any material form (including photocopying or storing it in any medium by electronic means and whether or not transiently or incidentally to some other use of this publication) without the written permission of the copyright owner, except in accordance with the provisions of the Copyright, Designs and Patents Act 1988.Applications for the copyright owner's written permission should be addressed to the publisher.

This is an independent publication and it is unofficial and unauthorised and as such has no connection with the artist or artists featured, their management or any other organisation connected in any way whatsoever with the artist or artists featured in the book.

Made in EU.
ISBN: 978-1-912918-85-0

Contents

Introduction

The meteoric rise of American singer-songwriter Billie Eilish is simply unprecedented. By the age of 22, she had done more in her five years at the top than most musicians manage over a lifetime's work.

She's become the ground-breaking artist of her generation and a global superstar, shattering expectations, rewriting the rules, and building an empire on close-to-mic, whispery vocals, haunting lyrics, and dark, intimate themes.

Since her 2015 breakthrough with viral hit "Ocean Eyes", she has gone on to smash record after record, most notably becoming the first artist born this century to have a #1 album in the US and to win a Grammy and two Oscars. In 2020, aged 18, she became the youngest artist, the first female artist, and only the second person in history to win all four major Grammy categories, including Album of the Year, for her debut *When We All Fall Asleep, Where Do We Go?* and Record of the Year and Song of the Year for "Bad Guy", the fifth single from that album, as well as Best New Artist, in a single ceremony.

Two years later she made history by becoming the youngest artist ever to write and record a theme song for the James Bond franchise, with "No Time to Die", which went on to win the Academy Award for Best Original Song in March 2022.

Teaming up once again with her brother Finneas she won a second Oscar in 2024 for Best Original Song with "What Was I Made For?" from the hit film *Barbie*, making her the youngest person to win two Academy Awards in any category.

Billie Eilish performs at Avicii Arena on April 23, 2025 in Stockholm, Sweden.

Beyond the charts and awards, Billie has made an indelible mark on pop culture. She's redefined fashion, embracing oversized silhouettes that challenged industry norms about female pop stars. She's been a vocal advocate for mental health, climate change, and body positivity, using her platform to inspire millions. Her ability to connect with fans on a raw, emotional level sets her apart in an industry often driven by spectacle. As she dives into debates on the causes she cares about - including animal rights, veganism, and Tourette's syndrome - she's become a poster-girl for Generation Z.

This biography unpacks a musical phenomenon—her inspirations, her struggles, and her unapologetic approach to fame. Whether you're a lifelong fan or just discovering her magic, this is Billie Eilish... revealed.

Billie Eilish performs her 'Hit Me Hard And Soft' Tour at Rod Laver Arena on March 04, 2025 in Melbourne, Australia.

Meet the O'Connells

'I've always done whatever I want and always been exactly who I am,' says Billie Eilish, the unique voice of Generation Z and currently one of the most influential pop stars on the planet.

Such a proclamation takes huge confidence - something you'd expect from a young woman whose unique brand of dark, experimental, pop-genre-defying music has earned her a global profile since her mid-teens. Yet, as a child, Billie's inner strength and self-assurance was buried beneath layers of sensitivity and separation anxiety which meant she would perform her first songs under a couch, hidden by cushions, and sleep in her parents' bed until she was 12. As she grew up she battled depression, body dysmorphia and self-harm.

What pulled her through all that, filled her with incredible strength and confidence, and provided a thorough grounding in music and song writing, was her slightly unconventional upbringing. Her parents Maggie Baird and Patrick O'Connell have always been actively involved with her career and remain massive pillars of support. Then of course there's her big brother Finneas, also her best friend and creative partner.

Billie's parents Maggie Baird and Patrick O'Connell are both actors who met in 1984 during rehearsals for a play in Alaska. They dated for 11 years before they got married in 1995 and based themselves in Los Angeles.

Maggie kicked off her career in 1981 as a supporting actor in the long running US soap opera *Another World*. Skilled in improvisation work, Maggie performed with Will Ferrell as part of the Groundlings troupe in Los Angeles in the mid-90s. She was also Melissa McCarthy's first improvisation teacher. Patrick has appeared on numerous hit TV shows including T*he West Wing* and *NYPD* and later in the 2008 hit movie *Iron Man*.

They decided to have children when they were slightly older than average - Maggie was 38 and Patrick 40. The couple conceived easily and Finneas was born in July 1997. However, having a brother or sister for him proved more difficult. So, the couple turned to a fertility clinic for help, and after four failed attempts, successfully had Billie four years later, on 18 December 2001. Billie didn't know the circumstances of her conception until she and the family were interviewed by US host Howard Stern in 2019. Having wheedled the information about the mechanics of working with a fertility clinic out of her parents during a rather excruciating exchange, Stern joked that Billie's unique talents could be because she was 'built in a lab'.

Having managed to complete their family with two planned and much wanted children, Patrick and Maggie decided they wanted to spend every possible moment with Finneas and Billie. Their brand of attachment parenting extended to co-sleeping with them and teaching them at home, rather than sending them to school.

The family's home in Los Angeles, California, was a two-bedroom, 1,200 sq. ft, ranch-style bungalow in the suburban neighbourhood of Highland Park, a creative area to the east of the city. In between acting jobs, Maggie and Patrick would supplement their income with other work, typically music and teaching for Maggie and carpentry and construction projects for Patrick. The couple slept on a futon in the living room because they thought it was more important that their son and daughter each had their own room to provide them with some private space.

While Maggie and Patrick always made a good enough living, LA is an expensive city so there were also a few tough times along the way. Most particularly in the mid-2000s, when the property market collapsed, the family lost almost everything because of a house 'flip' they were involved with. 'We were poor as f***' remembers Billie, who was six at the time.
Although the family was by no means on the breadline, holidays and luxuries were few and far between when Finneas and Billie were children. But what they may have lacked materially, they more than made up for in opportunities. Their loving and non-judgemental parents had few rules, preferring to give the children parameters around acceptable and unacceptable behaviour. 'There were no consequences and no rewards', as Patrick explains. 'No time-outs or punishments – we never really disciplined them'.

Billie Eilish, Finneas O'Connell, Patrick O'Connell and Maggie Baird attend Billboard Women In Music 2019, presented by YouTube Music, on December 12, 2019 in Los Angeles, California.

Being home-schooled by arty and creative parents, with no formal curriculum to follow, allowed young Finneas and Billie to express themselves in all sorts of ways -via music, art, dancing, singing, or making their own movies. Home-schooling meant that Finneas and Billie could do the things that they really loved to do and not have an academic schedule on top of it.

'Our whole stance was, general knowledge is all', Patrick explained once in an interview. 'You need to know why the sky is blue, but you don't need to memorize a bunch of esoterica you'll never use'.

'I wrote my first song at 12 and remember someone asking, "What were you going through at 12 that you could write about?" I get what you're saying, but 11, 12, 13 were the hardest years of my life. You learn everything. You learn how horrible things feel.'

Blessed with lots of freedom and time, the O'Connell children would explore whatever interested them that day or week; typically this would involve art classes, museums, or science programs at Cal Tech - the California Institute of Technology.

Music was the soundtrack of this happy life in LA. Maggie, who is also a singer, taught them the basics of song-writing, including verses, choruses, and chords. She remembers that Billie sang on pitch very early, including harmonies. There was always a piano or three in the living room which everyone would play and Finneas remembers 'music was in every nook and cranny of the house'.

As the elder of the two, Finneas was first to show his musical talents and his small bedroom became a home music studio. It's where he and Billie have created most of their music to date. As she grew older it was clear that Billie shared Finneas' musical interest and talent. Their parents let them get on with it, believing that what they were doing was important. So much so that when the siblings were making music of any description, separately or together, there was no bedtime. Music trumped everything.

Billie credits her parents for providing her with a brilliant musical education. Speaking to Apple Music's Zane Lowe in 2020 she said, 'My dad and I have had this relationship over the years of sharing music with each other. My dad has shown me some of my favourite songs in the world and I've shown him songs that he loves and adores also'.

Maggie and Patrick don't have much time for their own acting careers these days. Despite Billie's phenomenal success and consequent ability to employ whatever staff she might need, the whole family are still integral to the business side of her life, as well as the personal.

Having always been so closely involved with the children, neither parent needed to think twice before deciding to join them on the road when Billie began touring. In the early days Patrick drove the tour van and taught himself how to work the lighting. He's also a skilled carpenter so always found plenty to do. 'I thought, "When is this ever gonna happen again" ' he says. 'I wanted to be a part of it, because it's pretty darn cool'.

He's remained part of it - still integral to the tours and happy to muck in when needed. Maggie too is an important touchstone and gatekeeper for Billie, making sure she is well, safe and protected. Back in the pre-fame days, Maggie would fuel Billie and Finneas' music-making sessions with burritos and grilled cheese sandwiches - nowadays she's still on hand to make sure that Billie is eating well, and feeling well, especially amid the rigors of touring.

Mother and daughter are both amazed that other stars tour without similar family support. As well as looking after Billie, Maggie is also known for being 'mummy' to any of the crew on the tour when they need something.

When Finneas and Billie picked up their Oscar for Best Original Song with "No Time to Die", Finneas closed his acceptance speech by thanking their parents, saying they had always been, '...our inspirations and our heroes. We love you as parents and we love you as real people too'.

Enter Billie Eilish Pirate Baird O'Connell

When Billie was born on 18 December 2001, her big brother Finneas decided she would be called Pirate. Her parents, who have Scottish and Irish roots, had settled on Eilish, the Irish version of Elizabeth.

But in the end their daughter was named after Maggie's father William (Bill) Baird who died before Billie was born, and the other possible Christian names stacked up as middle names.

So, as Billie Eilish Pirate Baird O'Connell settled into her new life in Los Angeles, she found herself surrounded by a home filled with music and creativity. Perhaps it was inevitable that Billie would become a performer. Maggie was a keen singer - she released a country music album called *We Sail* in 2009 - the house was full of music and instruments and Finneas was already proving to be a talented musician himself.

Billie started playing the ukulele when she was six and used it when she wrote her first songs. One of the first songs she learned to play on the ukulele was "I Will" by the Beatles – a favourite band in her house.

Later Billie joined the Los Angeles Children's Chorus, a well-respected choir and choral music organisation, which taught her a lot about performance. Before gaining confidence with the choir, Billie would choose to sing her favourite songs while hiding under the pillows of the couch - "Happiness is a Warm Gun" from The Beatles' *White Album* was a favourite. Later she was brave enough to sing that same song at a home school talent show – an unusual choice from a child, but very typically Billie.

Artists like Linkin Park had a huge influence on Billie

'When people ask me, "When did you start singing?" I think that's a dumb question', Billie told *NME* in 2019. 'I was always singing and making up melodies and that was normal for our family to do that. I'd meet families who didn't do that and I'd think "what the hell?"'

But she became more serious about creating music when she was 11 and wrote her first 'real' song, which was about a zombie apocalypse. Music from acts like The Beatles, pop punk queen Avril Lavigne and teen star Justin Bieber - who was Billie's childhood crush - was played on repeat in her bedroom. She also loved Linkin Park, Green Day, and Lana Del Rey. Then she discovered hip hop which is still a passion these days and acknowledges artists such as rappers Tyler, The Creator and Childish Gambino as big influences on her own music. She also credits her home city of LA with playing a part in her success. As she told DJ Zane Lowe in the Disney+ concert film, *Happier Than Ever: A Love Letter to Los Angeles*, 'It formed me. It made me who I am and gave me the opportunities that I got. I don't think I'd have any of the same anything if it wasn't for my hometown'.

As might be expected from the daughter of actor parents, Billie also did her share of acting auditions, but never really thought it was the life for her. She did some background dialogue for crowd scenes in *Diary of a Wimpy Kid*, and *Ramona and Beezus*, but soon discovered that the acting world didn't appeal.

In fact, she is on record as declaring acting to be 'super-weird ...You can work for years and years and be the best in the world and never get a role, and you can be mediocre, do one audition, and become a huge star. For years, I saw my parents beat up over the fact that they didn't have it better. And that drove me insane – because they were really good! My dad is the best actor I've ever seen. And my mom can do all these voices and characters – she's incredible. So I wish they'd had more recognition'.

'Pretty much my whole life, I've been a performer and have loved singing and writing songs in my room for my own ears'.

Having ruled out an acting career, Billie thought that she would prefer to be behind the camera – at one stage her parents guessed she might become a movie director. When she was young she would borrow Patrick's digital camera and film little dramas starring her toy animals in the back garden. She then began making and editing home movies.

Another of Billie's childhood interests was horses. Because riding lessons were expensive and a luxury too far at the time, Billie began working at a local stable in exchange for lessons. She would happily spend hours grooming the horses to 'earn' some time riding and jumping them. Her favourite horse was a black mare named Jackie O, but she abruptly stopped riding her and going to the stables altogether after another girl, who didn't need to work to afford her riding lessons, took a fancy to Jackie O and began riding her regularly. Billie felt heart-broken, feeling that her special bond with Jackie O was broken. She stopped visiting the stables, deciding that she'd had enough of feeling second rate compared to the richer girls who didn't need to 'work' to afford to ride.

Luckily enough she had another string to her bow – her favourite hobby of all was contemporary dance. Billie was talented and a real prospect - in fact, a gambler would have put money on her making a living as a dancer at that time. Training for an average of 12 hours a week at the Revolution Dance Center on Honolulu Avenue in LA, Billie was incredibly focussed and seriously considered a career in dance. But those dreams were dashed when she was 13 and badly damaged her growth plate - an area of growing tissue at the top of her thigh bone - during an advanced hip hop class. Growth plate fractures affect how the bone will grow, with the worst-case scenario being a bone ending up more crooked or shorter than the opposite limb. Such an unexpected injury put paid to any chance of a career and her dance dreams evaporated almost overnight.

The setback was a massive upset in Billie's young life and one which led to her first bout of depression, including some self-harming behaviour. Speaking later, Billie said that her early teenage years, between 13 and 16 were 'rough times' and that she often thought she 'deserved to be in pain'.

The only upside to the whole horrible situation was that her schedule suddenly opened up, and she found more time to devote to her music. Looking back on it now the other benefit of giving up dance was that it helped her shift the focus away from her body issues – Billie has since said that this period in her early teens represented the peak time of her body dysmorphia.

Her always highly sensitive personality was partly explained when she discovered that she lives with a condition called synaesthesia. This is a neurosensory issue, affecting about four per cent of the population but more common in creative people. In lay terms, it means that the brain is "cross-wired" so that it comes to blend senses together. Billie will experience words as colours, for example, and can 'see' her music. As she explained to *Rolling Stone* magazine, 'Every person I know has their own colour and shape and number in my head, but it's normal to me'.

SUBPAC
SUBPAC

She went on to tell the magazine that she sees Finneas' entire being as an orange triangle, although his actual name appears as dark green to her. She experiences her monster hit single "Bad Guy" as 'yellow, but also red, while the number seven - it's not hot, but warm, like an oven. And it smells like cookies'.

Billie also lives with another neurological condition, Tourette's disorder, which means she can make unwanted, involuntary muscle movements and sounds, known as tics. Her symptoms are relatively mild, but sometimes she will bulge out her eyes or her head will twitch to one side.

Other young girls may have felt this was all enough to cope with, never mind forging a music career at the same time. But Billie uses her quirks to her advantage.

It's probably precisely because Billie copes with so many challenges of her own that her fans find her so relatable. Billie makes it clear she 'gets' them as well, for example telling the crowd at one gig; 'You guys all need to be ok, cos you're the reason I'm ok, ok?!'

Billie 'officially' moved out from home in 2019 but she hasn't gone far. She says that she still often spends the night in her childhood bedroom to be close to her parents.

Billie Eilish - Fact file

Height: 5ft 3.5 ins (1.61m)

Eye colour: Blue

Teenage crush: Justin Bieber

Musical influences: Tyler, the Creator, Donald Glover (Childish Gambino), Lana del Rey

Billie and Finneas on stage, Milan, Italy, 2019

Finneas

Singer-songwriter and record producer Finneas O'Connell is Billie's big brother and trusted collaborator.

Now known professionally by the mononym FINNEAS, he co-writes and produces Billie's music and is usually at her side during interviews and performances. The pair are extremely close and, arguably, she would not be where she is today without him.

Clearly blessed with outstanding talents of his own, there is frequent press speculation about how he copes with taking a back seat to Billie's front and centre position as a globally famous pop star. Yet she is there at his behest. Billie remembers him saying to her years ago that he intended to 'make her the biggest pop star' in the world.

Born on 20 July 1997, Finneas was a precocious child. According to his father Patrick he was early to talk and always happiest in the company of adults, rather than being with other children.

Billie and Finneas speak onstage at The 2018 ASCAP "I Create Music" EXPO at Loews Hollywood Hotel on May 8, 2018 in Hollywood, California.

Billie has said that she felt her older brother was the favoured 'golden child' for many years and that she was 'dragged' along to watch his performances at various events - he was a member of the Los Angeles Children's Choir before Billie joined. Her parents obviously deny having a favourite child, saying simply that Finneas is more like his mother in personality, whereas Billie is like her father.

Like Billie, he didn't go to a regular school but was taught at home by his parents. He has since spoken about it being a hugely positive experience. 'Being home-schooled is all about self-discovery', he told *Your Teen* back in 2014. 'It's something that I've really enjoyed and thrived under. I'm not at a high school where I have to base my self-worth off what other people think of me. I have to think, "What would I like to be doing? How would I like to be as a person?" I think that's an enormously positive thing'.

'Me and my brother get along super well. We're, like, best friends. So we'll stay up until, like, five just talking because we get along and, you know, it's cool. And he respects my opinions, and I respect his, even if we don't have the same opinions, but a lot of the time we do'.

Finneas asked for his first drum kit for Christmas at the age of three and also taught himself to play the piano. Maggie schooled him in the basics of song-writing and he was always keen on producing new sounds and experimenting with whatever equipment he had. 'I like to push things to their limits to see how much I can get out of each individual piece of equipment I have', he has said. He's also acknowledged that he was fortunate to be afforded the opportunities he enjoyed, including the resources of a computer and Logic Pro recording and mixing software, as well as being given the time he needed to perfect his skills.

But alongside his music, Finneas also had a shot at work as an actor. When he was 16 he appeared with his mother Maggie in a film she had co-written, inspired by her experiences at Open Mic nights. Called *Life Inside Out*, the film told the parallel stories of a mother called

Laura, played by Maggie, and her family, including troubled son Shane, played by Finneas, who find a powerful connection through their shared love and talent for music and song-writing.

Finneas went on to do some other acting work, most notably appearing in the 2011 hit comedy *Bad Teacher* with Cameron Diaz, and in a 2014 episode of hit US sitcom *Modern Family*. He also played Alistair, a member of the New Directions group, in the final series of *Glee* in 2015.

But by his mid-teens Finneas was pretty settled on working in music. His home studio was set up to his precise specifications and he was pushing his modest range of production equipment to its limits. For years he has worked at his computer, sandwiched in by keyboards either side of him, and often with Billie completing the 'square' sitting on his bed with a microphone.

'For me it's all about immediacy' he has said. 'The way I want any home studio to function is that as fast as I can think of an idea I want to be able to articulate it'. By the time he reached mid-teens, Finneas was lead singer and songwriter with his own alternative pop/ rock band called The Slightlys. On their behalf he put some feelers out into the industry and fortunately caught the attention of Danny Rukasin, co-founder of Best Friends music management company.

'I listened to the music he was writing and producing and I thought it exceptional – especially at his age of 16, 17', said Danny later in an interview with *Music Business Worldwide*. Danny offered some general advice for the band and introduced Finneas to a producer who worked with him on a handful of songs. The pair stayed in touch, and it was when Danny heard some of the music Finneas had begun to make with his sister Billie that things really started to happen.

Finneas – Fact file

Born: 30 July 1997

Height: 6 ft.

Girlfriend: Yes. In a relationship with YouTuber Claudia Sulewski since 2018

Finneas and Billie perform onstage at the 2020 iHeartRadio ALTer EGO at The Forum on January 18, 2020 in Inglewood, California.

Beginning in the bedroom...

As Billie grew up she began writing with Finneas more and more. Far from being an annoying little sister, she was an inspiration for him.

The pair began recording their songs on an iMac in Finneas' bedroom. Billie recorded most of her early vocals sitting cross-legged on the bed just a few feet away from Finneas at his desk.

Although they didn't realise it at the time, the bedroom gave them a very specific sound, tight and intimate, closed and quiet. It wasn't until they started recording elsewhere that Finneas appreciated the way his home set-up made the vocals sound - and it's a vibe that he always works hard to recreate when they record these days with many options at their disposal.

'Writing a song is so personal', said Billie, talking about collaborating with her brother. 'You have to have trust in someone you're working with; otherwise, you're not gonna come out with something that's really you'.

The siblings have said that they like to mix things up when they write. Sometimes they completely make up things and become characters so that their songs are entirely fictional, whereas at other times they will use their experiences as inspiration.

Finneas has said that he listens carefully to Billie's ideas, to help her tell whatever story she's trying to tell, using language that fits her voice.

As well as their obvious creative connection, the siblings share other traits which make them perfect partners. Both are extremely painstaking and don't care how long they spend on just one note in order to get it exactly right. They think outside of the box and use all kinds of sounds to boost and flavour their sound - for example standing in their bathroom lighting matches for hours to capture and later amplify the sound of the flaring.

Billie and Finneas perform during 'One World: Together At Home' presented by Global Citizen on April, 18, 2020

Finneas had gained great experience writing and producing with The Slightlys, but found new ideas and energy with Billie's input. For many years she has kept a notebook full of drawings and phrases which she comes back to for inspiration. By the time she was 13, Billie had song-writing skills to match her brother and things really took off. At first they would write separately then get together to work on the production. Their earliest collaborations include *"sHE's brOKen"*, written by Finneas, and *"Fingers Crossed"*, written by Billie, both of which they uploaded to SoundCloud, an early streaming and distribution platform.

'Billie has this specific vocal range, sort of between a whisper and a hum. If you play a lot of instruments in that range, her voice sounds foggy - but things like bass, kick drums, and low, clocky snares can co-exist and not conflict'.

After this, Fred Diaz, Billie's dance teacher at the Revolution Dance Center, who knew about her musical abilities, asked if she was interested in writing and performing a song which he would choreograph for the dance studio's next recital.

Up against it timewise, Billie was talking the project through with Finneas when he remembered a track called "Ocean Eyes" which he had written for his band The Slightlys. Realising that it would fulfil the dance brief, he also decided that the song was actually a better fit for Billie's voice. So, rather than save it for his band, Finneas helped Billie to remix and record it, using his production software.

In the song, Billie is talking directly to a love interest, praising his eyes as being as beautiful and mesmerising as the ocean. But although the lyrics speak of love, Billie and Finneas did not produce a traditional love song - there are hints of toxicity in the relationship, for example the lyric, 'No fair, You really know how to make me cry'.

The siblings released their track on SoundCloud, as was their pattern, with a free download link to make it easier for Fred to access it.

This turned out to be Billie's unexpected and massive breakthrough.

Her arresting delivery and ethereal vocals caused a big buzz as the track gained traction and received 1000 plays within 24 hours, and several hundred thousand listens within two weeks.

'We had no intentions for it, really,' Billie told *Teen Vogue* afterwards. 'But basically overnight a ton of people started hearing it and sharing it. Hillydilly, a music discovery website, found it and posted it and it just got bigger and bigger. It was really surreal'.

Billie Eilish, cultural phenomenon and alt-pop sensation in waiting, had taken her first step out of the bedroom and onto the world stage.

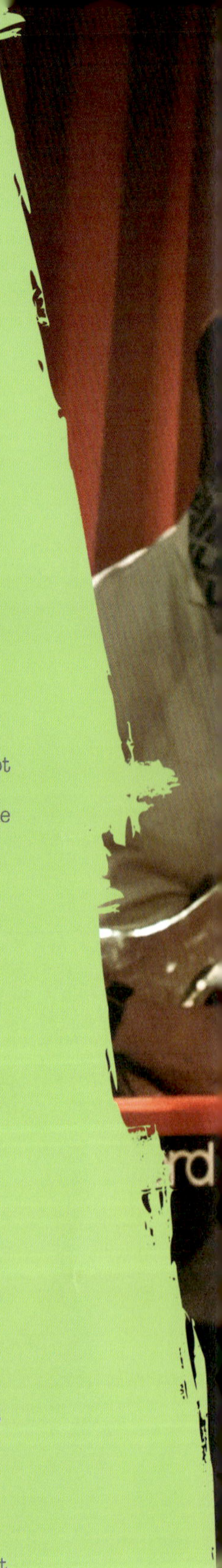

Billie Eilish performs live on stage during a concert at the Lido on February 26, 2018 in Berlin, Germany.

AKAI

Billie Eilish performs during day two of the Festival Corona Capital 2019 at Foro Sol on November 17, 2019 in Mexico City, Mexico.

Breaking through

2015-2016

'It happened really fast,' said Billie's dance teacher Fred Diaz, recalling those early days after "Ocean Eyes" went viral. 'One minute, it was a song she was going to dance to, and the next...' The song was a hit.

Fred did go on to choreograph a dance to "Ocean Eyes", and it was performed by students at Revolution in 2016. Sadly of course, Billie couldn't join in because this was all happening around the time of her hip problem. But in the event, the fame about to envelop her would mean that she would have no time for dance classes in any case.

Fred is still in touch with Billie and Finneas, who also took some classes with him as a child some classes with him as a child. 'We still talk about how crazy it was', Fred says. 'They still say, "Thank you," every time.' Finneas explained that eternal gratitude in an interview with *NME*, acknowledging that the SoundCloud upload for Fred opened the doors to their future success. 'It gave us something from nothing, which is so unbelievable,' he said. 'So I always have this profound gratitude for that song - obviously, our careers have been built on different moments since then, but that was the thing without which we never had anything'.

Following the SoundCloud release of "Ocean Eyes" in November 2015, people were knocked out by Billie's performance and potential and surprised to learn that she was only 13 years old. Danny Rukasin, already working with Finneas, was one of the first people to get in touch to discuss the best way of building on the incredible reaction to her performance of the song. In Danny's opinion, she could achieve significant success with help from Finneas.

"Ocean Eyes" drove all of us to take notice,' Danny told *MBW*. 'The next day I was with

Finneas and his family and with Billie, meeting everybody and talking about what they wanted to do. The song had already crossed into viral territory overnight. We discussed whether or not this was something Billie was really interested in doing or just a hobby, and we got to know and understand Billie. It was still early stages, but she had a vision of how she wanted what she was doing to be put out in the world. '

Billie remembers Danny telling her and Finneas; 'Dude, this is going to get huge and I think you're going to need help along the way. I want to help you guys'.

'Then we were like, "That's swag"'.

Within weeks, Danny worked with Finneas to make a deal with Apple Music and Platoon, an Artists and Repertoire (A&R) company specialising in supporting emerging artists who are ready to sign with a major label.

With that came a whole slew of support, including the engagement of a publicist and a stylist to work on Billie's image. In March 2016 Billie worked with director Megan Thompson to produce a music video for "Ocean Eyes", which premiered on her YouTube channel on 24 March 2016 to huge acclaim from radio stations and DJs including Zane Lowe, Jason Kramer and Annie Mac. The siblings made the most of subsequent opportunities from early features on Apple's Beats 1 and late-night TV.

Despite the dizzying swirl of activity around them, Billie and Finneas never lost sight of their music and found time to continue working on writing and producing tracks. They made a second single, "Six Feet Under," written by Finneas and again released through SoundCloud, and accompanied it with a homemade music video directed by Billie and edited by her mother, Maggie. This song was about reflections on a dead relationship and Billie's complicated

Eyeing up the video

The official music video for "Ocean Eyes" has since racked up over 537.7 million views on YouTube since it was published there on 24 March 2016.

Billie attends 14th Annual Teen Vogue Young Hollywood with American Eagle Outfitters on September 23, 2016 in Malibu, California.

thoughts about her ex – knowing things were over but still thinking about him and wondering what might have been. As the lyrics go: 'Our love is six feet under, I can't help but wonder, if our grave was watered by the rain, would roses bloom, could roses bloom again?'

Watching all this activity with interest was Justin Lubliner who had founded his own music company, The Darkroom, in 2014. Encompassing artist management and his own imprint in partnership with Interscope, the Darkroom Records label was a growing force in the industry. Also interested in music start-ups, Lubliner swooped in to sign Billie in August 2016. His plan was to model her launch on the path taken by hip hop artists such as Travis Scott and Chance the Rapper, by creating 'a persona and distinct aesthetic' rather than relying on one massive hit single to breakthrough.

Through Darkroom and Interscope Records, Justin re-released "Six Feet Under" and "Ocean Eyes" as singles for digital download and streaming in November 2016 – exactly a year after "Ocean Eyes" first attracted professional attention. Also that month Billie produced a dance performance music video of "Ocean Eyes" which she uploaded to her YouTube channel, giving the song a further lease of life.

'I don't know how to function without music. When I'm not making it, I'm listening to it. It gives me courage and takes care of my mind.'

Critics were overwhelmingly positive about the track, variously describing it as 'lush', 'heart breaking' and 'moody'. *Vogue* praised Billie's "airy soprano vocals [that] also conjure up thoughts of the ocean washing over the song's mellow percussion and minimalist synths', while *Atwood Magazine*, which focusses on emerging artists, attributed the lyrics, layered vocals and Billie's 'great voice' as what made the track so 'special'.

When Billie signed her first record deal, her new team of execs, perhaps naturally enough, assumed she would move her work out of her bedroom studio into their more professional facilities. They also offered her the opportunity to work with a team of very experienced writers and producers.

In typical Billie fashion she simply refused. 'I hated it so much,' she said later. 'It was always these 50-year-old men who'd written these 'big hit songs!' and then they're horrible at it. I'm like, "You did this a hundred years ago. Ugh"'.

So Billie and Finneas got their wish to continue writing and producing most of their own material, leaving others to mastermind the launch and advancement of their work. The *Music Business Worldwide* website described Billie's promotion from this point as 'a highly calculated, single-by-single release strategy with accompanying drops of merchandising, visuals and videos, all backed up by a precision plan for radio promotions and touring'.

Her growing management team - including Danny Rukasin, his Best Friends co-founder and Billie's co-manager Brandon Goodman, John Janick at Interscope, Justin Lubliner at Darkroom, and the live music agency Paradigm - carefully controlled the strategy. However, Billie was fully involved in every decision. The overriding aim was to build momentum carefully before releasing a full album.

'I do think that Billie would have had success regardless, as she's an incredibly talented and unique one-of-a-kind artist,' Brandon told *MBW*. 'But it's undeniable that we have seen so much value globally by having such a powerful system in place... people and partners that have worked tirelessly alongside us to make Billie arguably the most talked-about new artist'.

2017 began with the January release of an EP "Ocean Eyes - The Remixes" featuring artists Astronomyy, Blackbear, Goldhouse and Cautious Clay. This was followed up by another remix EP, this time of "Six Feet Under" by artists Blu J, Gazzo, Jerry Folk and Aire Atlantica.

Then in February came the release of a brand-new track, "Bellyache", written from the point of view of a conflicted serial killer. Billy said the track was more generally about guilt and that the 'bellyache' from the title refers to the stomach pains she would feel when she suffered guilt after stealing toys from her friends as a young child.

By setting the disturbing lyrics against an upbeat tune, Billie and Finneas earned some great reviews. For BBC News, Mark Savage said the song was the 'pop equivalent' to the works of acclaimed neo-noir move director Quentin Tarantino for finding 'comic absurdity in the midst of eye-popping gore'. Other reviewers said that the song confirmed Billie's 'precocious talent' and ability to craft 'perfect pop'. *Ladygunn* magazine made one of the first of what would come to be frequent comparisons with the unconventional style of Lorde, saying the track evoked, 'a darker Lorde over a trap-infused beat'.

As well as Lorde, music critics have also likened Billie's music to that of Lana Del Rey, for sharing an almost cinematic scope and for its exploration of tragic romance and melancholy. But Billie is quick to dismiss any such talk saying that Del Rey has 'made her brand so perfect for her whole career and she shouldn't have to hear that'.

Billie performs onstage during the Glamour Women Of The Year Live Summit at Brooklyn Museum on November 13, 2017 in New York City.

"Bellyache" made some commercial headway, spending 32 weeks and peaking at #3 on the US Bubbling Under Top 100 chart as well as making the top 100 on the UK, Australian and Canadian singles charts.

Following smartly after that came the singles "Bored" - lead single for the soundtrack to '13 Reasons Why' on Netflix - "Watch", and the anthem of anger that is "Copycat". Then on 14 August came her debut EP *Don't Smile at Me*.

Released on 11 August 2017, it featured an eclectic mix of seven tracks, which NME described as adding "a brash hip-hop edge to sugar-sweet pop".

Billie told *Billboard* magazine that the themes and links between the tracks were far from the typical pop trope. 'I'm pretty sure I don't have any songs that are about how much I love someone. They're all either about like, "I hate you," or "you make me hate me"'.

She also explained that the EP's title was chosen '… for a lot of reasons, but one of them would be when [someone tells you], "Smile. Why aren't you smiling? It's so much more beautiful when you smile." Everyone's taught to smile. Girls are like, "Look happy, look like you're having fun!" I'm not gonna look like anybody except what I am. I want to impress myself'.

Nevertheless, she did impress huge numbers of other people and the EP charted on the Top 20 in over a dozen countries including the US, UK, Canada, and Australia. In September 2017, Apple named her their newest Up Next artist.

The EP was a sleeper hit, reaching #14 on the US Billboard 200 chart. So it was promoted by a short tour of North America during October 2017. Prior to this - her debut headlining tour - Billie had made only brief forays into live performance, for example when Apple Music had showcased her at the South by Southwest music festival in March 2017.

● Billie Eilish performs at the 2018 Bonnaroo Arts And Music Festival June 9, 2018 in Manchester, Tennessee.

Don't Smile at Me Track list

Copycat
Idontwannabeyouanymore
My Boy
Watch
Party Favor
Bellyache
Ocean Eyes
Hostage
&burn

Billie was just 15 years old when she made this tour, so naturally her parents Maggie and Patrick had some concerns.

'When it first started, my biggest fear was that they would exploit her fast and be done with her', says Maggie. Thankfully, that didn't happen, but her parents remain vigilant, nevertheless. 'Her teenage years were wrested from her', Patrick has said. 'She was being shuttled all over the country at 14. That's *really* young. So although this has all been pretty wonderful and extraordinary, we try to put a buffer between Billie and the ravenous industry. Because it's too much'.

It was after this first tour that Billie first began to realise one of the downsides of fame – the inability to go out alone in public. In an interview with *V* magazine she described going ice-skating with a friend; 'It was a nightmare and it scared the living hell out of me because I was just turned into this prop. I've never been so scared. It was like a huge stampede...in those three months [of touring] I'd gotten bigger, but I didn't know it until I was in that situation. From that day on, I didn't go anywhere. I didn't do anything. I was so flipped out by what had happened and how powerless I felt. And I didn't have security because I didn't have the money for it. It was the level of fame that needs security, but also the level of fame where you don't really have the resources'.

Although Billie has posted about her fear of live performances, she has also described it as the 'best thing' and now says she much prefers shows to writing.

She's an energetic performer, famous for jumping around, something she always does, even once when she was injured and wearing leg splints.

Back from the tour, Billie released "Bitches Broken Hearts" on 10 November. Her team worked with Spotify which promoted her on its Today's Top Hits playlist, further expanding her reach and subsequent commercial success.

Billie Eilish attends the launch of The Coco Club celebrated by CHANEL at The Wing Soho on November 10, 2017 in New York City

CHANEL

Billie Eilish performs at the Central Presbyterian Church on March 16, 2017 in Austin, Texas.

Billie loves...

Driving – as a 17th birthday present from her record label Billie collected a Dodge Challenger called Dragon

Vegans – she's a life-long veggie and now vegan

Childhood pets – a rescue cat and dog called Misha and Pepper, and a new dog called Shark

Billie performs live on stage at The Anthem on June 20, 2019 in Washington, D.C.

Billie hates...

People she's not interested in – her father Patrick says she has no tolerance and doesn't care what people think of her

Horror films

Getting 'too old' – she believes that 27 is too old

As well as giving a further boost to pre-released hits such as "Ocean Eyes" and "Bellyache", the track "idontwannabeyouanymore" was released as a single and broke into the Billboard Hot 100 at #100. It was written by Billie and Finneas about Billie's periods of depression, and she sings about her self-doubt and issues around negative self-esteem.

Although this was a subject she understood well, more generally Billie doesn't believe that she needs to have experienced everything she writes about, saying, '[People] feel like you have to write about what you're going through, and how you feel, and it can't be anything else – and that's just so untrue. You don't have to be in love to write a song about being in love. You don't have to hate someone to write a song about hate. Writing music is just like writing a book'.

Don't Smile at Me was some debut - a best-seller of a 'book' with many of its tracks still included in her setlist today.

Billie arrives for the premiere of the film 'Everything Everything' in Hollywood, California on May 6, 2017

The *Don't Smile at Me* concert tour was in support of Billie's debut EP *Don't Smile at Me* and consisted of 11 dates in North America in October 2017.

October 2017

04	Constellation Room	Santa Ana
05	The Echo	Los Angeles
07	Rickshaw Stop	San Francisco
09	Holocene	Portland
10	The Crocodile Back Bar	Seattle
12	Schubas Tavern	Chicago
14	Drake Hotel	Toronto
16	Baby's All Right	Brooklyn
19	Sonia	Cambridge
20	World Café Live	Philadelphia*
21	Rock & Roll Hotel	Washington, D.C.

*Philadelphia set list:

Copycat
Idontwannbeyouanymore
Watch
Six Feet Under
Hotline Bling
Party Favor
I'm In Love Without You
Listen
Ocean Eyes
Wish You Were Gay
Bellyache

Worldwide fame

2018

In February 2018, Billie embarked on her second headlining concert tour, the 28-date Where's My Mind tour of Europe, North America and Canada. Finneas backed her on stage and performed his own number, "New Girl".

Pride burst out from Maggie and Patrick, watching from the wings, as their children were welcomed on stage every night with a volley of excited screams from the crowd.

As Billboard magazine wrote in its review of her show at the Bowery Ballroom in New York City, Billie's performance, by turns tender and exciting, was 'the type of show where you are acutely aware that the artist you are currently watching will outgrow the venue they are playing almost immediately'.

By now Billie was well into her stride as a performer, showing a natural talent for commanding the stage and engaging with her audiences. She had begun to use her trademark moves of flicking her hair, sticking her tongue out, and jumping around for the more energetic numbers. She has said that she feels at her most powerful when she is on stage. 'I am the best that I can be on stage. If I go on in a bad mood I come off stage completely rejuvenated'.

The review of her London concert by music website *The Line of Best Fit* noted that her performance was; 'Genius, bewitching and powerful, not only because of Eilish's talent, but the devotion, love and passion of all the fans in that room'.

Billie Eilish performs live on stage during a concert at the Lido on February 26, 2018 in Berlin, Germany.

The Where's My Mind concert tour was also to support Billie's Don't Smile at Me EP and consisted of dates in North America and Europe in Spring 2018.

February 2018

14	Heaven	London, UK
16	Petit Bain	Paris, France
18	Dude Club	Milan, Italy
19	Debaser Strand	Stockholm, Sweden
20	Melkweg	Amsterdam, Netherlands
23	Botanique/Rotonde	Brussels, Belgium
26	Lido	Berlin, Germany
27	Jungle Club	Cologne, Germany

March 2018

01	By:Larm	Oslo, Norway
07	El Rey Theatre	Los Angeles, USA
08	Great American Music Hall	San Francisco, USA
10	Music Box	San Diego, USA
11	The Observatory	Santa Ana, USA
17	Terminal West	Atlanta, USA
20	Black Cat	Washington D.C., USA
21	Coda	Philadelphia, USA
23	Bowery Ballroom	New York City, USA
24	Paradise Rock Club	Boston, USA
26	Bowery Ballroom	New York City, USA
27	Theatre Fairmount	Montreal, Canada
28	Mod Club Theatre	Toronto, Canada
30	El Club	Detroit, USA
31	Lincoln Hall	Chicago, USA

April 2018

03	First Avenue	Minneapolis, USA
04	recordBar	Kansas City, USA
06	Bluebird Theater	Denver, USA
07	The Complex	Salt Lake City, USA

Billie Eilish performs a live concert at Sentrum Scene during the Norwegian showcase festival and music conference By Larm 2018 in Oslo.

'I don't want people at my shows to come out and say, "I just saw a cool show." I want them to say, "I had fun at the show." I want it to be a collaborative thing and be part of the audience and have them be part of me. I try to interact with everyone there and have them be equal to me because they are'.

The set included a backdrop of a huge metal spider which glowed in different colours to match the music. Dressed in black versions of her trademark oversized t-shirt and knee-length shorts combo, Billie played her ukulele during "Party Favors" and joined the audience in jumping around for the more upbeat tracks. Then she was captivating during the quieter numbers and at one point stopped the action to ask the audience, '...for the next song I would like everyone to put their phones away and focus on me, like it's just me and you in the room, it's me, you, and the music'.

Within months, by early January 2019, *Don't Smile at Me* reached 1 billion streams on Spotify, making Billie the youngest artist to top 1 billion streams on a project.

Her profile was boosted when Florence & the Machine asked Billie to support them on some of their *High As Hope* world tour dates. Billie opened for them in October 2018 in Nashville and Charlotte during breaks in her own *1 by 1 Tour*, another to support her *Don't Smile At Me* EP.

The reviews for the tour raved about her energy, her power and ability to almost hypnotise an audience as she ran about the stage, jumped on the speakers and reached out to fans all while delivering a note-perfect performance.

The world was ready for more of Billie and her genre-defying music. Time for an album release....

Billie Eilish performs during the 2018 Okeechobee Music Festival at Sunshine Grove on March 3, 2018 in Okeechobee, Florida.

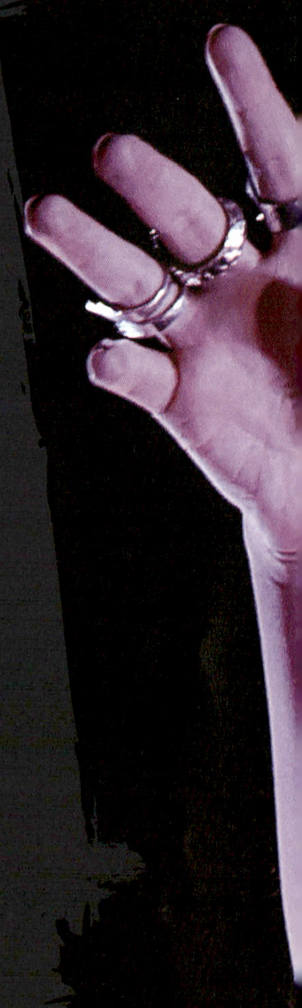

The 1 by 1 concert tour was also to support Billie's *Don't Smile at Me* EP and consisted of dates in North America and Europe in the autumn/winter of 2018-19.

October 2018

20	Fox Oakland Theatre	Oakland, USA
21	Ace of Spades	Sacramento, USA
23	Roseland Theatre	Portland, USA
24	The Showbox	Seattle, USA
28	Metro	Chicago, USA
30-31	Phoenix Concert Theatre	Toronto, Canada

November 2018

02	House of Blues	Boston, USA
03	Irving Plaza	New York City, USA
04	Union Transfer	Philadelphia, USA
05	Brooklyn Steel	Brooklyn NYC, USA
07	9.30 Club	Washington D.C., USA
09	Variety Playhouse	Atlanta, USA
13	Granada Theater	Dallas, USA
14	Emo's	Austin, USA
16	The Van Buren	Phoenix, USA
17	Soma	San Diego, USA
20-23	The Fonda Theatre	Los Angeles, USA

February 2019

11	Kesselhaus	Berlin, Germany
12	Uebel & Gefahrlich	Hamburg, Germany
13	Vega	Copenhagen, Denmark
15	Fryshuset	Stockholm, Sweden
17	Gibson Club	Frankfurt, Germany
18	La Cigale	Paris, France
21	Fabrique	Milan, Italy
22	Halle 622	Zurich, Switzerland
24	TivoliVredenburg	Utrecht, Netherlands
25	Salle de la Madeleine	Brussels, Belgium
27	Manchester Academy	Manchester, UK
28	SWG2 Studio	Glasgow, UK

March 2019

02	02 Institute 1	Birmingham, UK
04-06	02 Shepherd's Bush Empire	London, UK
09	Sala La (2) De Apolo	Barcelona, Spain

Billie Eilish performs in concert at Sant Jordi Club stage on March 9, 2019 in Barcelona, Spain.

Billie Eilish performs during the Bonnaroo Music and Arts Festival on June 9, 2018 in Manchester, Tennessee.

A stunning debut album

2019

To the uninitiated, Billie's phenomenal success with *When We All Fall Asleep, Where Do We Go?* would seem to come out of nowhere, yet she had actually been releasing music for a full three and a half years before this debut full-length album dropped.

As well as waiting to ensure that the demand was there, Billie and Finneas had also waited until they had a cohesive body of work - songs that creatively fitted together and that were designed to be listened to as a whole - rather than just put out a collection of different tracks.

When it came to recording this first album, Billie decided to rely on her tried and trusted approach of working in the bedroom with Finneas, singing into a mic while sitting on his bed, as she had for all her previous music.

'It's crazy. Most people need to stand and open their diaphragms, but Billie sounds amazing just slumped on the bed', Finneas has observed.

The pair co-wrote 11 of the 13 tracks, while Finneas alone contributed "When the Party's Over" and "My Strange Addiction" as well as handling all the production. Working only when they felt like it, sometimes for short bursts and other times staying up all night, the siblings noted their progress on a chart in the room where they had previously marked their growing heights as children.

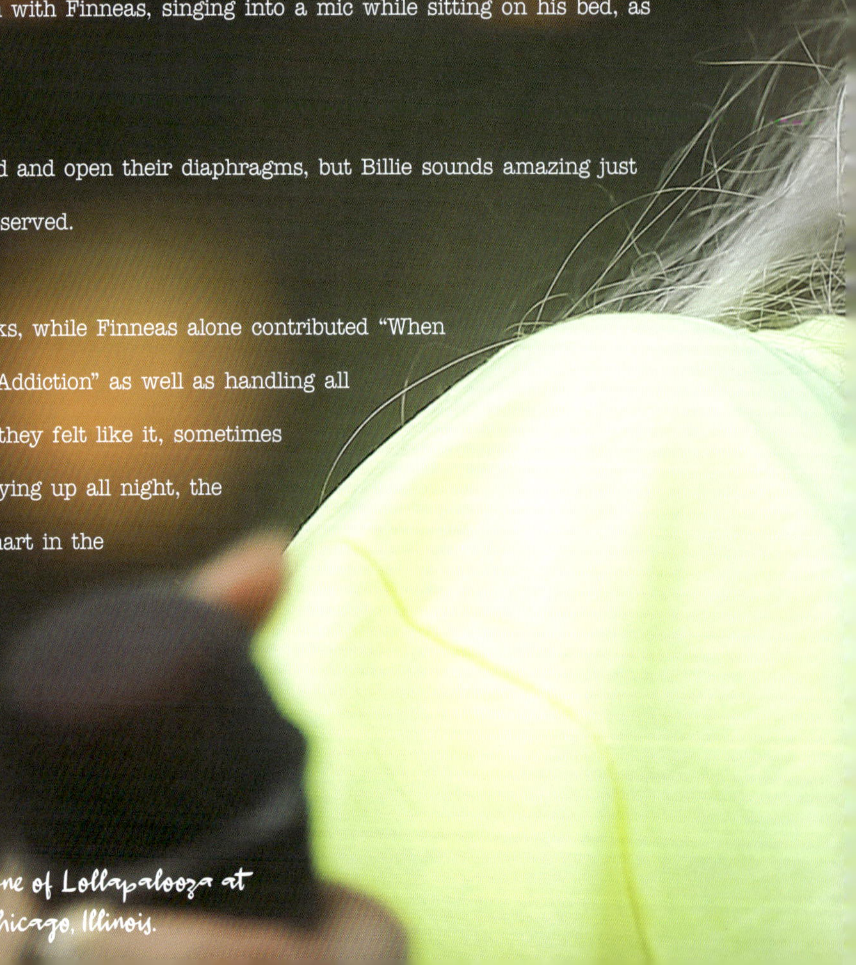

Billie Eilish performs on day one of Lollapalooza at Grant Park on August 2, 2018 in Chicago, Illinois.

A stunning debut album (2019)

When We All Fall Asleep, Where Do We Go?

Release date: 29 March 2019
Record label: Darkroom/Interscope

Track list

!!!!!!!
Bad Guy
Xanny
You Should See Me In A Crown
All the Good Girls Go to Hell
Wish You Were Gay
When the Party's Over
8
My Strange Addiction
Bury A Friend
ilomilo
Listen Before I Go
I Love You
Goodbye

The album's theme was sleep; more specifically things that can happen when you're sleeping - which in Billie's case includes sleep paralysis, night terrors, nightmares, lucid dreams. All things that don't have an explanation. All things nobody can really explain, as Billie told Beats 1 host Zane Lowe. 'I've always had really bad night terrors and sleep paralysis, and all my dreams are lucid, so I can control them—I know that I'm dreaming when I'm dreaming. Sometimes the thing from my dream happens the next day and it's so weird. The album isn't me saying, "I dreamed that"—it's the feeling.

In the same interview Finneas spoke of his pride that he and Billie hadn't shied away from songs about self-loathing, insecurity, and frustration, saying, 'Because we feel that way, for sure. When you've supplied empathy for people, I think you've achieved something in music'.

They certainly had. Finally available on 29 March 2019, their debut album *When We All Fall Asleep, Where Do We Go?* became one of the best-selling albums of the year, and among the most successful debut albums of all time.

Tracks from the album released ahead of its launch, including "You Should See Me in A Crown" in July 2018 and "When the Party's Over" in October 2018 had helped spark incredible levels of anticipation for this new music. The videos accompanying these tracks were phenomenal and attention grabbing. Billie cried black tears in "When the Party's Over" and was toying with tarantulas in "You Should See Me In A Crown"

Having already become the most pre-added album of all time on Apple Music (800,000 globally), within days Billie's debut album was number one on the Billboard 200, with 313,000 equivalent album sales in its first week. It also made #1 in the UK, giving Billie the distinction of becoming the youngest ever solo female act to top the album chart. By July 2019 the album had been streamed over 2 billion times.

This album also saw Billie break the record for the most songs by a female artist simultaneously charting on the Hot 100 - 14 in total - after every track from the album except "Goodbye" made the chart.

The reviews were phenomenal as critics widely acclaimed the work. In the US, online music site *Pitchfork* described the album as [living] 'in a world of its own: gothic, bass-heavy, at turns daring and quite beautiful', while entertainment site *Vulture* said 'Her music resonates because she is able to articulate the absurdities of the young American experience with wit, tenderness, and brutal honesty. Her debut album is a quiet revolution, both intricate and also delicate, sweet but sometimes prickly, like berries in a bramble. *When We All Fall Asleep, Where Do We Go?* is frequently stunning and doubly so for a debut album by someone not even old enough to vote'. *Variety* credited the album's use of dissonance and distortion as supporting its success, commenting that, 'With all its moments of distortion and attitude, tempered by sheer loveliness, and rude and emotional songs about night terrors and daydreams, *When We All Fall Asleep, Where Do We Go?* feels like a rock 'n' roll album, even if there's virtually nothing on it that sounds like rock music'.

'Words are more powerful than some noises. Noises won't last long. Lyrics are so important, and people don't realize that'.

Billie Eilish performs on stage at Marymoor Park on June 02, 2019 in Redmond, Washington

In the UK, *The Guardian* newspaper voted her 'Artist of the Year' and its music critic Alexis Petridis said the album 'confirmed her as the most exciting pop artist of her age: a dark, adventurous, eclectic set of songs, that appeared blithely unconcerned with chasing trends'. Of those 'trends' the one towards artists releasing single tracks as playlist fodder for streaming platforms was the most 'bucked', as Finneas and Billie always intended the songs on their album to be consumed one after the other as a 'whole'.

Featuring electronica, bass-heavy pop, piano and even ukulele, their debut proved impossible to categorise and shattered the idea that the concept of a cohesive album had been killed by the streaming platforms. On the day of its release Apple Music found that 81 per cent of the album was played through by its listeners - a particularly impressive achievement set against the estimate that generally only 16 percent of UK adults listen to an album from start to finish.

Billboard Woman of the Year - 2019

Billie was named Woman of the Year 2019 by Billboard, who said 'Billie has disrupted the entertainment industry through her music and social media platforms, leaving an indelible impact on the global cultural zeitgeist.'

'I listen to music all day every day. I can't not listen to music. It's kind of scary how much I listen to music, but it's what I love, and it's all I care about, so I'm good with it'.

As an intro, Billie announces she is taking out her braces and she and Finneas dissolve into giggles before the first track proper kicks in. Her pronouncement, 'I have taken out my Invisalign and this is the album' segues into the album's stand out track and fifth single "Bad Guy", which, as well as boosting album sales, gave Billie her first number-one hit on the Billboard Hot 100.

Their attention to detail on the album was off the scale. For example, on "Bad Guy" Finneas famously used the sound of an Australian road crossing as a metronomic beat and Billie reportedly did 34 takes of the word 'doh', although it is seemingly thrown in casually before the main instrumental riff takes off.

The cover for the album was a photograph of Billie taken by veteran photographer Kenneth Cappello, who had produced the cover photograph for *Don't Smile at Me*.

The now iconic image shows Billie, dressed in white and sitting on a white bed, smiling demonically, her eyes glowing white, minus pupils, like a shot from a horror film. All is dark and unsettling, apart from Billie and the bed which starkly emerge from blackness. A nightmarish image which was reportedly inspired by the bad dreams and night terrors Billie suffers herself. She brought sketches and concepts along to the shoot to show Kenneth what she wanted to achieve.

Billie Eilish attends the 2019 Billboard Women In Music at Hollywood Palladium on December 12, 2019 in Los Angeles, California.

'I know if I'm going to work with Billie, we're going to make cool stuff,' Kenneth told *MTV News*. 'I knew she wanted it moody. And I wanted it to feel real, obviously. I wanted it to feel like a door was opening and that was the light coming into the bedroom, like from another room. Kind of spotty. And that's not [post-production]; everything is lit in camera'.

Billie's white eyes were also not a post-production gimmick, she wore contacts that completely covered up any colour in her eyes. 'She goes all in on everything', continued Kenneth who first met Billie when he took the cover shot for *Don't Smile At Me* when she was just 15 years old.

'I was like, "She can't be 15". Not because of the way she looks, but the way her mind works. She's kind of a step ahead of her age [because of] her thought process, the way she holds herself as a person, the way she speaks, and the way she knows exactly what she wants and she's not going to waver around that'.

The tour to promote the album kicked off at the Coachella Festival in California on 13 April 2019 and ran until 17 November 2019. Compared to her relatively humble tour beginnings - when the O'Connell family would allocate $100 a night for a stay in a budget hotel - Billie's fifth tour was as big-scale as they come. She was now a huge star and needed the bells and whistles that come with performing in big areas to huge audiences around the world, and the travel schedules this demands. It was nerve wracking and Billie has said that she struggled to get her head around this level of fame and did experience some panic attacks before the tour began.

But none of that showed once she got on stage. Because Billie's syneasthesia makes her such a visual person, she sets her music to amazing images during her concerts, including fantastic lightshows.

This show opened in suitably dramatic style when a doll laying on a bed, apparently sleeping, suddenly sat up as Finneas and their drummer came on stage, as if it had woken from a bad dream. It was a rather creepy set up which delighted fans before Billie and the rest of the band arrived and launched into "Bad Guy".

● Billie Eilish performs at Outdoor Theatre during the 2019 Coachella Valley Music And Arts Festival on April 20, 2019 in Indio, California.

Playing Coachella

One of the many special moments captured in *The World's A Little Blurry* documentary comes when Billie played the Coachella music festival at the start of her *When We All Fall Asleep* world tour and had a surprise meeting with her childhood idol Justin Beiber. Despite being one of the most famous music stars in the world, Billie is shown absolutely awe-struck and unusually speechless as Bieber appears in front of her.

Billie Eilish performs at Outdoor Theatre during the 2019 Coachella Valley Music And Arts Festival on April 13, 2019 in Indio, California.

The 'When We All Fall Asleep' world tour in support of When We All Fall Asleep, Where Do We Go? consisted of 66 dates in North America, Oceania and Europe between April and November 2019.

April 2019

13+20	Empire Polo Club (as part of Coachella)	California, USA
24	Spark Arena	Auckland, NZ
26	Adelaide Showground	Adelaide, Australia
27	Maitland Arena	Maitland, Australia
28	Exhibition Park	Canberra, Australia
30	Hordern Pavilion	Sydney, Australia

May 2019

03	Margaret Court Arena	Melbourne, Australia
04	Prince of Wales Showground	Bendigo, Australia
05	Murray Sports Complex	Townsville, Australia
07	Riverstage	Brisbane, Australia
10	Fremantle Arts Centre	Fremantle, Australia
11	Hay International Park	Bunbury, Australia
25	Stewart Park	Middlesborough, UK
29	Bill Graham Civic Auditorium	San Francisco, USA
31	Moda Center	Portland, USA

June 2019

01	PNE Amphitheater	Vancouver, Canada
02	Marymoor Park	Redmond, USA
04	The Great Saltair	Magna, USA
05	Red Rocks Amphitheater	Morrison, USA
07	Silverstein Eye Centers Arena	Independence, USA
08	Minneapolis Armory	Minneapolis, USA
09	United Center	Chicago, USA
11	Budweiser Stage	Toronto, Canada
12	Place Bell	Laval, Canada
14	Leader Bank Pavilion	Boston, USA
15	The Met Philadelphia	Philadelphia, USA
18	Rooftop at Pier 17	New York City, USA
19	Radio City Music Hall	New York City, USA
20	The Anthem	Washington, USA
21	Ascend Amphitheater	Nashville, USA
23	State Bank Amphitheatre	Atlanta
27	Tusindarsskoven	Odense, Denmark
28	Gardet	Stockholm, Sweden
30	Worthy Farm (Glastonbury)	Pilton, UK

July 2019

06	American Family Insurance Amphitheater	Milwaukee, USA
09/10	Shrine Exposition Hall	Los Angeles, USA
11	Greek Theatre	Los Angeles, USA
13	Cal Coast Credit Union Theatre	San Diego, USA

August 2019

15	Green Park	Sankt Polten, Austria
16	Hamburg-Wilhelmsburg	Hamburg, Germany
17	Walibi Holland	Biddinghuizen, Netherlands
18	Kempische Steenweg	Hasselt, Belgium
20	02 Arena	Prague, Czech Republic
22	Glattbrug	Zurich, Switzerland
24	Reading Festival	Reading, UK
26	Leeds Festival	Leeds, UK
27	Megasport Arena	Moscow, Russia
28	Ice Palace	St Petersburg, Russia
30	Stradbally Hall	Stradbally, Ireland
31	Area Expo	Milan, Italy

September 2019

02	Palau Sant Jordi	Barcelona, Spain
03	WiZink Center	Madrid, Spain
04	Altice Arena	Lisbon, Portugal
07	Olympiapark	Berlin, Germany
14	Piedmont Park	Atlanta, USA
20	Downtown Las Vegas	Las Vegas, USA
21	Las Vegas Festival Grounds	Winchester, USA

October 2019

05	Zilker Park	Austin, USA
07	BOK Center	Tulsa, USA
08	American Airlines Center	Dallas, USA
10	Toyota Center	Houston, USA
12	Zilker Park	Austin, USA

November 2019

17	Autodromo Hermanos Rodriguez (Corona Capital)	Mexico City, Mexico

Billie Eilish performs in support of her *When We All Fall Asleep, Where Do We Go?* release at Bill Graham Civic Auditorium on May 29, 2019 in San Francisco, California.

BILLIE EILISH

At one point, Billie told the audience about how she generally sat on a bed at home when she was writing with Finneas and said that she would like to perform that way too. Then the siblings climbed onto a bed which was raised above the stage as they sang.

Discussing her experience of watching her children move from singing in their bedroom to performing before huge crowds in massive arenas, their mother Maggie told interviewer James Corden, 'It has never not been mind-blowing. It blew my mind even when I sat here [in the bedroom] and heard Billie and Finneas play a song. It's never not been mind-blowing, you know? The whole experience is so crazy'. Renowned for always encouraging her children's talents, Maggie agreed that whenever they played her their music she would ask, 'When is it going to come out?' because she wanted Billie's songs to be heard by 'everyone in the world'. Now that is really happening, she said, 'I can't describe it because it's too amazing'.

The album's success was also charted in the Apple+ TV film *Billie Eilish: The World's a Little Blurry*, directed by R J Cutler. Taking a deep dive into Billie's personal life, it follows her rise to fame from her first tour with the EP *Don't Smile at Me*, through to the release of "Bad Guy" and *When We All Fall Asleep, Where Do We Go?*, also including home movie footage from her childhood years.

As director Cutler told *Los Angeles Magazine*, like many young people of her generation, Billie's life is almost completely documented. 'There was a GoPro on a tripod in a bedroom and if the kids felt inspired, they turned it on... If there was a meeting or a conversation or a song, their mother would turn on her iPhone and film. She's seeing things only a mother can see and you're getting this remarkable mother's perspective'.

He added that his 2.5 hour film provided viewers with an 'observational lens, storytelling with no filter, filming performances as intimately as possible' and providing 'a rich opportunity for us filmmakers'.

In an interview with US host Stephen Colbert, Billie said the doc isn't 'everything ... like, you're seeing a sliver of my life at that time ... there's a ton that isn't in there, but it's pretty much me'.

Fans hold up homemade signs of Billie Eilish's face waiting for her to perform live at Marymoor Park on June 02, 2019 in Redmond, Washington.

The documentary was released on 26 February 2021 when it won plaudits from critics and fans alike for its 'honest' and 'engaging' coming of age storytelling. As Cutler told Sky News, 'It's very rare to see an artist at that level of achievement in the actual process of creation and all its challenges, its conflicts, its obstacles'.

By the end of 2019, *When We All Fall Asleep, Where Do We Go?* had sold more than 1.2 million pure copies worldwide, making it the fifth best-selling album of the year and the third best-selling by a female artist. Its success made Billie the fourth best-selling artist of 2019.

When the end of year album rankings were published, *When We All Fall Asleep, Where Do We Go?* appeared on numerous lists of 2019's top albums, topping many of them. As well as naming the album the best of 2019, influential music critic Robert Christgau also ranked it as the fourth best album of the entire 2010 decade, saying of Billie, 'No teenager I can recall has ever made such an impressive album'.

The album was evidently going to take some beating. But the follow up was going to have to wait… James Bond had come calling.

Mission accomplished

Just a few carefully chosen artists are honoured with a request to create and perform a James Bond theme. The phenomenally successful, 60-year-strong movie franchise is universally acclaimed and the accompanying lead song for each film is always keenly anticipated.

Producers can, and do, take their pick from the very best singers and songwriters of the moment and past performers include established stars such as Shirley Bassey and Tom Jones, and, more recently, chart superstars Sam Smith and Adele.

So when a call came through asking if Billie and Finneas would be interested in writing the theme for the 25th James Bond film *No Time to Die* it was a dream come true. The answer was an immediate yes.

Billie and her whole family had been massive fans of the James Bond franchise for years. Even as children Billie and Finneas would do a song-writing exercise which involved constructing a song to the boundaries and challenges of a Bond theme - never guessing they would one day do it for real. Billie told Jimmy Kimmel in an interview that "Skyfall" by Adele was one of her favourite songs in the world, as well as her favourite Bond theme and film.

Working as usual with Finneas, Billie co-wrote and performed the song when she was aged 18, making her the youngest artist in history to record a theme for the Bond franchise.

Their song came together quickly. It was written in three days during a trip to Texas in October 2019 - based on a small section of the script which had been sent to them - and recorded as a demo inside their tour bus. Finneas said that after they'd finished composing the song, the pair

● Billie Eilish attends the *No Time To Die* World Premiere at The Royal Albert Hall on September 28, 2021 in London, England.

Other soundtrack hits

Billie's track *Bored* featured on the soundtrack of teen drama series Dead Girls' Don't Lie and *Lo Vas a Olvidar*, recorded with Spanish singer Rosalia, became the soundtrack of HBO series Euphoria.

listened to all the previous themes to, '...make sure that we weren't making something that just felt like we were copying other great songs'.

They weren't – they had come up with a masterpiece all their own. The demo went to Hans Zimmer, the composer of the movie's score, in December and once he was on board Billie and Finneas went to London to work with him, recording the song with a 70-strong orchestra. The whole process was extremely collaborative as Billie, Finneas and the Bond team worked together for the next few weeks, perfecting the song.

Up until this point the work had been conducted in the utmost secrecy. Then, after teasing fans on social media with a series of photographs of former Bond girls to suggest her involvement, Billie was officially confirmed as the singer of the 25th Bond theme by the movie's producers Michael G. Wilson and Barbara Broccoli on 14 January 2020. 'We are excited to announce that Billie and Finneas have written an incredibly powerful and moving song for *No Time to Die*, which has been impeccably crafted to work within the emotional story of the film,' they said. The film's director Cary Joji Fukunaga, a huge self-confessed fan of Billie and Finneas added: 'Their creative integrity and talent are second to none and I cannot wait for audiences to hear what they've brought - a fresh new perspective whose vocals will echo for generations to come'.

For her part, Billie tweeted: 'It feels crazy to be a part of this in every way. To be able to score the theme song to a film that is part of such a legendary series is a huge honour. James Bond is the coolest film franchise ever to exist. I'm still in shock'.

At that time the movie – which was actor Daniel Craig's last outing as the famous spy - was scheduled for release in the forthcoming April.

However, the Covid 19 pandemic put paid to that plan and the film was held back for a cinema release which didn't happen until the autumn of 2021. Billie's song of the same name, "No Time to Die", had been released in February 2020 – a full 20 months earlier – giving the composition the strange, and unwelcome, distinction of clocking up the longest time between the launch of a theme song and the release of the accompanying movie itself.

The delay meant that Billie and Finneas couldn't really talk much about their song, its mood, the ideas behind it and their lyrics, for fear of giving away information about the movie - the plot and themes of which were fiercely guarded secrets.

But there was still plenty of buzz around the understated ballad they had composed. Shrewdly, it maintained the sibling's trademark off-centre style throughout and was unmistakeably 'an Eilish production' despite its romantic overtones.

In an astute and respectful nod to their predecessors, the pair included several of the film series' musical motifs in their orchestration. Although they used the now traditional wooshes of strings and brass - and closed with the famous minor 9th chord from the original Bond theme - the composition was unmistakeably their own, incorporating the emblematic dark, electro-pop elements which had made them stars.

Lyrically, tho song references the career of James Bond and the deaths which his 'licence to kill' had occasioned in the past with the line; '*The blood you bleed is just the blood you owe*'. Later in the song, Billie sings '*Was I stupid to love you? / Was I reckless to help?' / Was it obvious to everybody else/That I'd fallen for a lie?*' putting herself in the position of a Bond girl questioning her involvement with the 007 spy.

'What makes a song last is real content from a mind that is thinking a little bit harder about certain things. A lot of artists don't really think that hard'.

Billie Eilish attends the World Premiere of the James Bond 007 film *No Time to Die* at the Royal Albert Hall in west London on September 28, 2021

The theme song won instant acclaim from critics and fans. In America, "No Time to Die" debuted at number 16 on the American Billboard Hot 100. The track was an even bigger hit across the Atlantic in the UK, scoring the biggest opening week of all time for a Bond theme, going straight to number one and amassing 10.6 million streams. As well as giving Billie her first UK number one, the song's success also made her the first artist born in the new millennium, the first female singer of a Bond theme, and only the second artist ever, to top the chart with a Bond theme.

Despite their iconic standing in the music and movie worlds, only one of the previous 25 Bond themes, Sam Smith's "Writing's on the Wall", had made it to number one, until Billie and "No Time to Die" topped the charts.

The accolades continued rolling in when the composition won the Grammy for Best Song Written for Visual Media in March 2021 and the Golden Globe for Best Original Song in January 2022.

Then came the biggest prize of all – an academy award. What was just a dream when they wrote James Bond themes for fun as children, became real in March 2022 when Billie and Finneas won the Oscar for Best Original Song.

'This is so unbelievable I could scream', said Billie. She and Finneas were clearly both overjoyed as they came on stage to collect their award. Although "No Time to Die" was the third Bond theme to win an Oscar, it was the first winning Bond theme to have been written by Americans.

The siblings also performed their song at the ceremony, giving an intense and polished rendition minutes before their win was announced. There was no doubt that they had fulfilled their 007 assignment.

Variety magazine in the US crowned "No Time to Die" the best Film Song of the Year 2021. Collecting the award at the 5th annual Variety Hitmakers award ceremony, Billie said, 'This is an honour. This was the most surreal song to be able to make and I can't thank everybody enough for letting me be a part of it'.

Billie Eilish and Finneas, winners of the Oscar for Original Song for 'No Time To Die' at the 94th Annual Academy Awards March 27, 2022 in Hollywood, California.

Variety also placed No Time to Die in its top ten of 'best-ever' Bond themes, with the following review:

'File this one in the Dept. of Controversial Choices made good… very good. The peasants were revolting when Eilish was first announced as the woman to send Daniel Craig off: Was a then-18-year-old really the delivery system to put us in mind of a Bond who's sailing, or bleeding, off into the sunset? Yet she and brother Finneas came up with the subtlest Bond theme in its five-decade history, but one not so subtle that Hans Zimmer didn't have good reason to incorporate into his instrumental music again and again, so much more so than usual that the O'Connell siblings nearly deserve score co-credit.

'The elements of betrayal – written specifically to emotionally wrap up the 25-minute (!) pre-credits sequence – feel wisened enough in Eilish's hushed delivery that you want to check her publicity still after the film to make sure she didn't develop wrinkles writing the song. It's to their credit that she and Finneas finally gave in to including echoes of the "James Bond Theme" along the way and didn't think adding that final "spy chord" was as corny as they feared it was, because the song was gloomily strong enough not to be undercut by a bare hint of fun'.

This level of success has brought her to the attention of a whole new and older demographic. She's now an artist beloved by her peers, but equally likely to feature on the playlist of their parents and grandparents.

No Time to Die, the movie, had its world premiere at the Royal Albert Hall in London on 28 September 2021, and was released in cinemas on 30 September 2021 in the UK and on 8 October 2021 in the US after the delay.

Billie and Finneas attended the star-studded red-carpet launch in London and met stars of the film, alongside royals the Prince and Princess of Wales, then the Duke and Duchess of Cambridge, William and Catherine. 'They were just so normal', Billie said afterwards. 'They didn't make me feel like, oh, I'm scared, I can't talk to them. They were like very complimentary, and they had all these questions for me. They were just very friendly and funny and sweet. I can't complain, it was amazing'.

Billie won fashion plaudits for the head-to-toe Gucci outfit she wore that night- a three-piece black co-ord, jacket, blouse and trousers, shimmering with gold thread and accessorised with gold jewellery and a pair of Gucci retro platform sandals in matelasse leather. Fans were also treated to a glimpse of a new tattoo - a fairy on her left hand.

What the critics said about Billie and Finneas' song "No Time to Die"

Pitchfork (US)

'...[the lyrics] reflect the betrayal hinted at in the film's trailer and embody the tension of espionage'.

BBC (UK)

'Easily the most audacious and atmospheric take on the Bond theme in recent memory'.

The Independent newspaper (UK)

'One of the best we've had in some time. The flourish of violins, electronic guitar and faint brass all pay tribute to classic Bond theme tropes, but Eilish's subtle synth motif makes this song her own. What makes it "Eilish" is that ever-so subtle but effective synth motif that runs in between the piano chords on the intro – a 2020 twist that marks "No Time to Die" as perhaps the only Bond theme that addresses how technology has changed things for both Bond and the music industry'.

Vulture (US)

'... a study in contrasts. It's possibly the quietest Bond song ever, while also being one of the few times you get to hear Eilish raise her voice to a shout, as she does when the strings swell at the song's climax. It's sparse-sounding and also lushly arranged....proof they do bells and whistles just as well as empty space and whispers'.

The Guardian newspaper (UK)

'No Time to Die' is a 'confident', and 'appealing addition to the Bond theme canon....A Bond theme befitting of the Craig era. The pop sensation [Billie Eilish] sidelines her trademarks for a tasteful track that matches the haunted solitude of its leading man'.

The Telegraph (UK)

'Eilish's "downbeat noir is spine-tingling".'

Plaudits and pandemic

Billie was just 18 years and 39 days old when she achieved a milestone five awards at the 2020 Grammys, including winning the four main categories, 'Best New Artist', 'Record of the Year', 'Song of the Year' (both for "Bad Guy") and 'Album of the Year' (*When We All Fall Asleep, Where Do We Go?*) - making her the youngest person and first woman to do so all in the same year.

Her fifth award was for 'Best Pop Vocal', while Finneas also picked up the Grammy for 'Producer of the Year, Non-Classical' - both for *When We All Fall Asleep, Where Do We Go?*

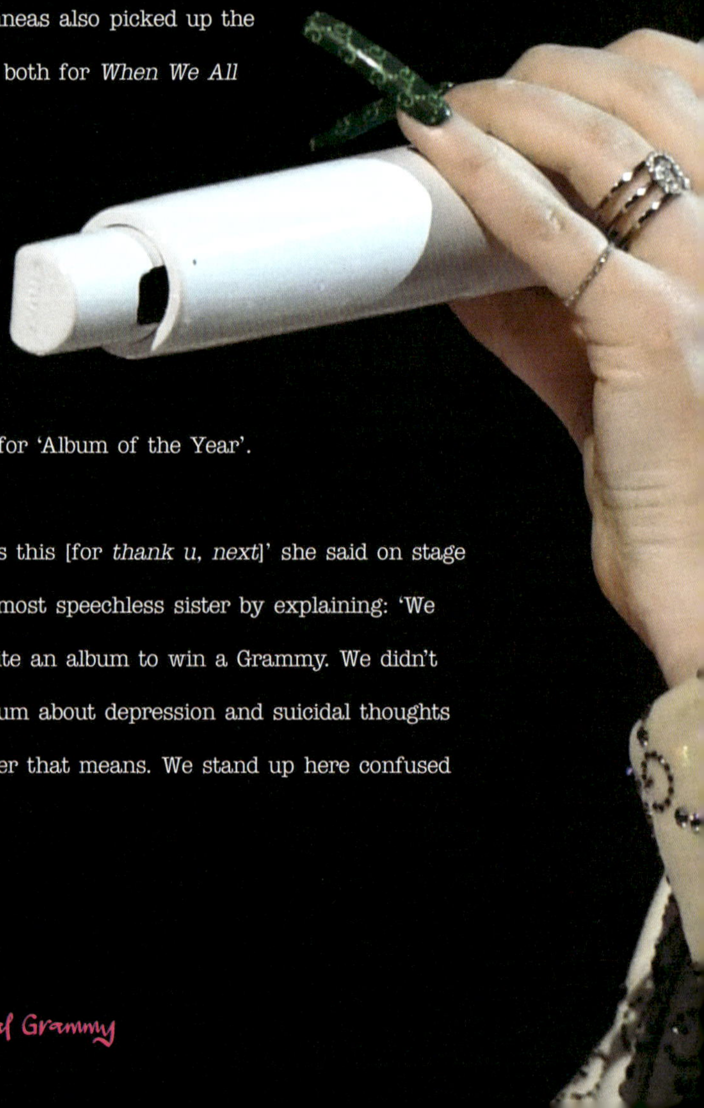

Despite such record-breaking success, Billie and Finneas were very humble about their success that night. Looking almost embarrassed, Billie was spotted by cameras mouthing 'Please don't be me' before her fifth win of the night, this time for 'Album of the Year'.

'Can I just say that I think Ariana Grande deserves this [for *thank u, next*]' she said on stage after collecting her statuette. Finneas helped his almost speechless sister by explaining: 'We didn't write a speech for this because we didn't write an album to win a Grammy. We didn't think it would win anything ever. We wrote an album about depression and suicidal thoughts and climate change and being the bad guy, whatever that means. We stand up here confused and grateful'.

Billie Eilish performs during the 62nd Annual Grammy Awards on January 26, 2020, in Los Angeles.

Just days after the Grammy awards on 26 January 2020, the global Covid 19 pandemic began to hit hard. Within weeks lockdowns began, with citizens all over the world told to stay at home.

This meant that Billie had to bring her fifth tour, a sell-out, to an abrupt halt three dates in. The *Where Do We Go?* world tour had opened in Miami on 9 March and been scheduled to run until 27 July, taking in North and South America, Europe and Asia. However on 16 March, after completing two further shows in Orlando and Raleigh in the US, Billie had to postpone the remainder of the opening North American leg due to the pandemic. Then on 13 May the rest of the tour was postponed and by 3 December all dates were officially cancelled, and tickets refunded.

During the pandemic Billie and Finneas continued writing and also performed at several 'virtual' charity concerts raising awareness and money to help defeat the virus and support crew members who were losing out on work. Then, possibly wishing to escape from the gloom of the illness and consequent isolation suffered by people all around the world, Billie's next single was rather more uplifting than most of her earlier recordings. "My Future", was written about a month into the lockdown and, as Billie told fans, it reflected where her head was at the time. Having used the lockdown to do some self-reflection and personal growth, Billie felt hopeful and excited about the future, as the lyrics explain.

The song was released on 30 July 2020 as the first single from her forthcoming second album. It entered the Billboard Hot 100 at #6 and made the top 10 and top five in charts around the world. It was streamed 20.9 million times and had 15,000 downloads in the US for the week beginning 31 July 2020.

The next single was "Everything I Wanted" which went on to win Record of the Year at the 2021 Grammy Awards. Despite its upbeat opening line, the song was inspired by a nightmare Billie had involving her jumping off the Golden Gate Bridge and dying.

● Billie Eilish and Finneas pose in the press room with their 5 Grammy Awards on January 26, 2020, in Los Angeles.

Billie wanted to put her feelings and fears into a song, but she had been so unsettled by the vision and other nightmares she suffered that her family became concerned about her wellbeing. Finneas said that he felt uncomfortable about the song and so helped Billie to change her idea and move away from a subject matter of depression and suicide, and instead to write about the sibling's strong relationship, how Finneas would always protect her from harm and about their mutual support for each other. In the accompanying music video Billie and Finneas are seen in a car driving through LA before veering off and sinking into the ocean.

Other singles released before the album came out were "Therefore I Am" and "Your Power", each making the top 10 both sides of the Atlantic. Once again the anticipation for a second album was at fever pitch.

In the meantime, the accolades kept coming as Billie took home three Billboard Music Awards in October 2020 - for Top Female Artist, Top New Artist and Top Billboard 200 Album (for *When We All Fall Asleep, Where Do We Go?*).

Billie Eilish and Finneas perform onstage at the 2020 iHeartRadio ALTer EGO at The Forum on January 18, 2020 in Inglewood, California.

NIKE
PSNY

Happier Than Ever

Billie's follow up album, *Happier Than Ever*, was mostly written during the 2020 Covid lockdown and charted the path of self-discovery she had taken during that time. Speaking afterwards in an interview with V magazine Billie said, 'I did so much self-reflection and thinking about my life and remembering my life, and going back to therapy and talking through my life. A lot was realised'.

Asked whether being a celebrity had been as restricting as it had been freeing, Billie replied that it was 50/50. 'There are so many things that I would never ever be able to do if I didn't have what I have, and so many things that I can never do again,' she said.

The fruit of this time and reflection was a collection of 16 songs, all co-written and produced by Finneas and released in July 2021 as the album *Happier Than Ever*.

The pair hadn't attempted to repeat the successful 'formula' of their first album but instead had opted to explore different styles and approaches, even referencing bossa nova and jazz vocals. Now famous and feted, they were coming to their song writing from a very different place, which naturally impacted on their reference points.

As *The New York Times* said in its review of the album, the opening track, "Getting Older" exemplifies this well; 'The song is a snapshot of Eilish's psyche on the other side of her titanic, arms-full-of-Grammys fame, and its particular flavour of top-of-the-mountain ennui somehow finds the aesthetic common ground between Drake and Peggy Lee. Strangers and stalkers clamour for Eilish's attention, which leaves her feeling more distant from the people around her. The music she used to make for fun has become a high-pressure job. "Things I once enjoyed," she croons with an is-that-all-there-is sigh, "just keep me employed now"'.

● Billie Eilish performs onstage during the 2021 iHeartRadio Music Festival on September 18, 2021 at T-Mobile Arena in Las Vegas, Nevada.

Happier than Ever

Release date: 30 July 2021
Record label: Darkroom/Interscope

Track list

Getting Older
I Didn't Change My Number
Billie Bossa Nova
my future
Oxytocin
GOLDWING
Lost Cause
Halley's Comet
Not My Responsibility
Overheated
Everybody Dies
Your Power
NDA
Therefore I Am
Happier Than Ever
Male Fantasy

Whereas before Billie's rarely raised her voice above a whisper, on this album, particularly on the title track, its volume is about the loudest it has ever sounded on record.

Happier Than Ever was highly anticipated and Apple Music said that more listeners added it to their libraries pre-release than had happened with any other album.

The reviews were generally four-star and praised the craftsmanship of the work, which proved Billie was no 'one-hit wonder'.

Acknowledging she now had a post-fame outlook, the *New York Times* said the album was, '... a record fixated on the tension between private and public knowledge, a social-media-era pop star's meditation on how much candour - if any - she owes her audience.... Eilish's body, her sexuality and her romantic relationships have all become targets of scrutiny as her fame has grown, and *Happier Than Ever* finds her erecting barbed boundaries around all these battle zones'.

The Forty-Five music website described the album as existing 'entirely on its own terms, apathetic about following mainstream trends or generating big hits' with the songs 'darker than ever'. Pitchfork said it was, 'woozy, effortlessly melodic, and showcases her command over the pop landscape'.

Rolling Stone magazine said the album was 'self-assured' and in the UK *The Guardian* described the album as 'bold and classy'.

As pandemic restrictions were lifted Billie was able to hit the road again to promote her album. *Happier Than Ever, The World Tour* began on 3 February 2022 in New Orleans and ran until September, taking in Canada, UK, Europe, Australia, and New Zealand as well as the USA. One of her biggest American gigs was in New York's Madison Square Garden. Afterwards in an interview with tv host Seth Meyers, Billie agreed that the date had blown her mind, saying, 'Yes I did bawl on stage. I did. It was just really weird. I have a song during the set where it's all baby footage of me. And I was walking across the stage, looking at baby me, looking at the crowd and I bawled. Quite embarrassing'.

Posters advertising the new album *Happier Than Ever* by Billie Eilish on 10th August 2021 in London, United Kingdom.

Seth replied that 'I don't think your audience minds when you get a little emotional?' and Billie agreed, 'No they love it....The fan connection has been the number one priority since literally the beginning. I wouldn't want to do any of this without it. I'm dead serious. There is no reason to do any of this without the connection. Literally, no reason at all'.

Of course Billie Eilish tours are a very different operation these days. It's reported that half a million tickets were sold for the *Happier Than Ever* tour in the first hour they went on sale. Finneas told *The New York Times* that despite the small-scale and sparse elements of Billie's music, they were unconcerned about taking the show to enormous venues such as New York's Madison Square Garden and the 02 in London with capacities of 20,000 plus. 'Billie's crowd is a real singalong crowd, so no matter how quiet the song is there's going to be 20,000 kids screaming the whole time,' he said.

The cheap motels of the early family trips are a distant memory, replaced by luxury air travel and tour buses. Maggie arranges for Billie's friends from home to visit the tour to try and keep her life as steady as possible. Similarly, Billie is very mindful of the safety and happiness of her sell-out concert audiences, even to the extent of stopping her performance if she spots anything amiss in the crowd so that anyone who's unwell or over-excited can be taken to safety.

Happier Than Ever, The World Tour Dates - 2022

North America

February 2022

03	Smoothie King Center	New Orleans, LA
05	State Farm Arena	Atlanta, GA
06	Spectrum Center	Charlotte, NC
08	PPG Paints Arena	Pittsburgh, PA
09	Capital One Arena	Washington, DC
10	Bryce Jordan Center	University Park, PA
12	KeyBank Center	Buffalo, NY
13	Wells Fargo Center	Philadelphia, PA
15	Centre Bell	Montreal, QC
16	Scotiabank Arena	Toronto, ON
18/19	Madison Square Garden	New York, NY
20	TD Garden	Boston, MA
22	Prudential Center	Newark, NJ

March 2022

08	Legacy Arena	Birmingham, AL
09	Bridgestone Arena	Nashville, TN
11	Yum! Center	Louisville, KY
12	Little Caesars Arena	Detroit, MI
14	United Center	Chicago, IL
15	Xcel Center	St. Paul, MN
16	CHI Health Center	Omaha, NE
19	Ball Arena (formerly Pepsi Center)	Denver, CO
21	Vivint Arena	Salt Lake City, UT
24	Rogers Arena	Vancouver, BC
25/26	Climate Pledge Arena	Seattle, WA
29	Chase Center	San Francisco, CA
30	Golden 1 Center	Sacramento, CA

April 2022

01	T-Mobile Arena	Las Vegas, NV
02/04	Gila River Arena	Glendale, AZ
06	The Forum	Los Angeles, CA
08/09	The Forum	Los Angeles, CA
16	Coachella	Indio, CA
23	Coachella	Indio, CA

Billie Eilish performs onstage during her Happier Than Ever tour opener at Smoothie King Center on February 03, 2022 in New Orleans, Louisiana.

Making a stand

Billie surprise-released the two-track EP *Guitar Songs*, featuring "TV" and "The 30th" in July 2022. The track "TV" was written in response to the decision of the U.S. Supreme Court a few weeks earlier to remove the constitutional right to abortion by overturning Roe v. Wade.

Billie was one of numerous artists to use their fame and platform to show disapproval of the decision. Billie's contribution was a track with powerful lyrics about how modern media provided distraction while fundamental rights were being stripped away and it resonated deeply with her fans.

Happier than Ever – typical set list

Bury A Friend
You Should See Me in A Crown
My Strange Addiction
Ocean Eyes
Copycat
When I Was Older
Wish You Were Gay
Xanny
Lighthouse
The Hill
The Approaching Night
Lovely
Listen Before I Go
I Love You
Ilomilo
Bellyache
Idontwannabeyouanymore
No Time to Die
When The Party's Over
All The Good Girls Go to Hell
Everything I Wanted
Bad Guy

Europe

June 2022

03	SSE Arena	Belfast, UK
04/05	3Arena	Dublin, Ireland
07/08	AO Arena	Manchester, UK
10-12	The O2	London, UK
14	The SSE Hydro	Glasgow, UK
15	Utilita Arena	Birmingham, UK
16	The O2	London, UK
18	Ziggo Dome	Amsterdam, Netherlands
19	Festhalle	Frankfurt, Germany
21	Lanxess Arena	Cologne
22	Accor Arena	Paris, France
24	Glastonbury Festival	Somerset, UK
25/26	The O2	London, UK
28	Sportpaleis	Antwerp, Belgium
30	Mercedes-Benz Arena	Berlin, Germany

July 2022

02	Hallenstadion	Zurich, Switzerland

Australasia

September 2022

08-10	Spark Arena	Auckland, New Zealand
13-15	Qudos Bank Arena	Sydney, Australia
17-19	Brisbane Entertainment Center	Brisbane, Australia
22-26	Rod Laver Arena	Melbourne, Australia
29-30	RAC Arena	Perth, Australia

December 2022

Billie concluded her *Happier Than Ever tour* with three concerts titled *Happier Than Ever, The Hometown Encore* at her local venue, the Kia Forum in Inglewood, California on December 13, 15 and 16.

● Billie Eilish performs onstage at The Kia Forum on December 13, 2022 in Inglewood, California.

Fearless about fashion

Billie's distinctive visual flair has long played a part in fixing her image in the public consciousness. She initially became known for her trademark over-sized and colourful androgynous co-ords – a type of uniform she adopted to prevent people from discussing her body because she wanted to be judged by her music rather than her look, size or shape.

By choosing oversized clothing, Billie felt she could help to maintain some privacy. In Calvin Klein's 2019 'I Speak My Truth In #MyCalvins' campaign, she said, 'Nobody can have an opinion because they haven't seen what's underneath, you know?'

Having once been subject to online criticism of her body, Billie now speaks out about 'body shaming' and once told *Vogue* magazine that it had been the initial reason for her depression when she was young. She made a video about the topic in 2020, called *Not My Responsibility*, during which she removes various items of her clothing and criticises 'watchers' for judging her body without asking, saying in a voice over:

'Though you've never seen my body, you still judge it – and judge me for it. Why? Why make assumptions about people based on their size? We decide who they are... Is my value based only on your perception or is your opinion of me not my responsibility'.

● Alicia Keys guest-hosts *The Late Late Show with James Corden* airing Monday, December 9, 2019, with guests Ali Wong and Billie Eilish.

Billie Eilish attends The 2021 Met Gala Celebrating In America: A Lexicon Of Fashion at Metropolitan Museum of Art on September 13, 2021 in New York City.

She has always appreciated the effect that clothes have on her well-being, saying that 'Clothing and fashion are kind of my security blanket, almost. If I'm in a bad mood, or if I'm uncomfortable, it's probably what I'm wearing that's making me feel that way'.

Known principally for her eccentric goth aesthetic, Billie now experiments with all different looks. Famously she wore an Alexander McQueen corset on the front cover of *Vogue* and when hosting the prestigious Met Gala in New York in September 2021, she wore an extravagant dress by Oscar de la Renta – on the condition that the brand would stop using real animal fur in its designs.

As her mother Maggie once said, 'the whole point of fame is to change the world for the better'.

Recently Billie has been combining more high fashion designer pieces into her red carpet wardrobe, while continuing to be a fashion disruptor. At the 2023 Met Gala she wore a dramatic, goth-inspired, black lace gown, featuring intricate beadwork and a flowing train, by Alexander McQueen.

She then chose Chanel for the 2024 Oscars ceremony, leaning into a 'schoolgirl' aesthetic with a white blouse, black jacket and a tweed pencil skirt teamed with knee-high white socks and classic black Mary Jane heels.

Scent of success

Billie's synaesthesia means that she has long experienced her thoughts and ideas in colours and scents, so a fragrance range was a natural extension of her brand. 'I've always had a severe connection to scent, and I remember everything through scent', she says.

In November 2021 she debuted her perfume 'Eilish', which developed into variants 'Eilish No 2' and 'Eilish No 3'. Then in February 2025 came her fourth fragrance 'Your Turn' – a unisex blend including ginger and sandalwood. Of course all her scents are vegan, cruelty-free, and made with clean ingredients.

Billie Eilish attends The 2022 Met Gala Celebrating "In America: An Anthology of Fashion" at The Metropolitan Museum of Art on May 02, 2022 in New York City.

Billie is also famous for changing up her hair colour. She's tried everything from light lavender to platinum blonde, gaining probably the most attention with her famous neon green roots. She's also fond of wearing a beanie hat and sunglasses.

She describes her style nowadays as 'anything goes' and advises people to 'wear what you want'. For Billie that also includes incredibly long, coffin-shaped acrylic fingernails.

'I just like dressing out of my comfort zone,' she told *Harper's* Bazaar in 2017. 'I want to dress in a way that if I was in a room full of people wearing regular clothes, I would be like, "Oh, I bet everyone's looking at me." I want to feel that way. That's my casual'.

Billie Eilish arrives for the 92nd Oscars at the Dolby Theatre in Hollywood, California on February 9, 2020.

In a Barbie world

Billie's contribution to the *Barbie* movie soundtrack in 2023 turned out to be bigger than anyone expected – it was Oscar winning.

The buzz around the 2023 movie *Barbie* was insane. Directed by Greta Gerwig and starring Margot Robbie as Barbie and Ryan Gosling as Ken, it was highly anticipated and did not disappoint, going on to be among that year's top films, a cultural phenomenon, and a huge critical and commercial success, grossing over $1.4 billion worldwide.

Alongside its innovative storytelling and visual appeal, the film's success is also attributed to its carefully curated soundtrack, featuring a diverse array of artists, blending pop, rock, and indie genres to complement the film's vibrant aesthetic. But the standout track was Billie's "What Was I Made For?"

This poignant ballad, written by Billie and Finneas especially for the film, absolutely captured the story's introspective moments and was lauded for its emotional depth as its melancholic tone mirrored the journey of Barbie's character in the film, who faces a personal crisis and starts questioning her place in the world. The lyrics delve into themes of self-discovery and existential reflection, aligning with the movie's broader themes and touches on the idea of transformation and embracing one's true self. This introspection is a central element of the *Barbie* film's narrative, and the song helps elevate that emotional journey.

The song was widely praised for its haunting beauty and emotional resonance, with Billie's ability to blend vulnerability with a larger-than-life cinematic experience impressing many. Fans and critics alike recognised the track for adding a layer of authenticity and sincerity to the Barbie movie's larger-than-life aesthetic. It offered a reflective moment that contrasted with the colourful, whimsical tone of the rest of the Barbie experience

Billie Eilish attends the World Premiere of *Barbie* at Shrine Auditorium and Expo Hall on July 09, 2023 in Los Angeles, California.

Money matters

In 2020 Billie became the youngest person to feature on the Forbes Celebrity 100 list, with earnings of $53million and rising.

While she makes most of her money from her recordings and live performances, her worth has been massively boosted recently by income from documentaries and books, endorsements and product launches such as her fragrances.

"What Was I Made For?" was not only a standout on the Barbie soundtrack but also performed very well commercially, topping various charts, including making #1 in the UK and gaining millions of streams within days of its release.

But its pivotal position in Billie's discography was underlined by the song's win at the 2024 Academy Awards where it won the Oscar for Best Original Song.

This marked a huge milestone in her career, as well as making Academy Award winning history. With a second win (after "No Time to Die" in 2022) Billie became, at age 22, the youngest double Oscar winner in history. The second youngest is now her 26-year-old brother and co-writer Finneas. The siblings also have a 100 per cent track record after two wins from two nominations.

Billie and Finneas performed "What Was I Made For?" during the 2024 Academy Awards ceremony, which was a memorable moment of the night. Their appearance was widely praised for its intimacy and simplicity, with Billie delivering the song with raw emotion.

'I'm so grateful for this song and for this movie and the way that it made me feel', Billie said during her acceptance speech. 'And this goes out to everyone who was affected by the movie and how incredible it is. And I want to thank my team and my parents. I love you guys so much'.

The song also won Grammy and Golden Globe awards, among many others, and featured on multiple Best Songs of 2023 lists. All this success, together with the Oscar, has solidified Billie's status as a versatile artist, capable of crafting songs that transcend genres and resonate on a global scale.

Arresting acting debut

In March 2023 Billie made her acting debut, guesting in the Amazon Prime Video black comedy/horror series *Swarm* which delves into the complexities of fan culture and the darker aspects of human obsession.

Her portrayal of Eva, a cult leader, received many positive reviews and won her a People's Choice Award for Performance of the Year 2024.

Discussing the role, Billie said that she found the portrayal of fan culture in *Swarm* both 'scary' and 'beautiful'. She remarked on the intense passion fans have, noting that 'Fans are really, so powerful, and I think maybe they don't realise how powerful they are'.

Swarm's co-creator Donald Glover who cast her told *Rolling Stone* that Billie '...understands storytelling at such a young age. And she's authentic to her experience. I feel she's living life for herself'.

Still of Billie from the series SWARM, season 1, ep.104, aired March 17, 2023

Billie Eilish (R) and US singer-songwriter Finneas O'Connell perform "What Was I Made For?" onstage during the 96th Annual Academy Awards at the Dolby Theatre in Hollywood, California on March 10, 2024.

Hit Me Hard and Soft

In 2024, Billie returned to the music business and the charts with her third studio album *Hit Me Hard and Soft*.

Released on 17 May it entered the US Billboard 200 chart at #2. In fact all 10 songs from the album made their debut in the top 40 of the Billboard Hot 100, giving Billie a career total of 43 charted songs. The physical version of the album topped the Vinyl Albums chart, giving Billie a 27 week total on the chart, second only to Taylor Swift. In the UK the album debuted at #1, marking the biggest opening week of her career with 67,100 chart units.

With more than six billion streams on Spotify, it became her fourth project to hit that number.

No tracks or teasers were issued ahead of the album as Billie and Finneas wanted it heard as a 'whole'. As Billie told *Rolling Stone*, '..every time an artist puts out a single without the context of the album, I'm just already prone to hating on it'.

Produced again by Finneas, the album showed that the siblings were continuing to push boundaries. Showcasing Billie's growth as an artist, the album displayed a sonic maturity as it blended her signature hushed vocals with intricate production and deeply personal lyricism.

Billie Eilish performs her *Hit Me Hard And Soft Tour* at Rod Laver Arena on March 04, 2025 in Melbourne, Australia.

The 'hard and soft' elements of the title came from the mix of emotional, introspective moments with uplifting sounds and innovative production. "Lunch", an infectious, bass-heavy, sapphic-focussed anthem was the first single release and made the top five, a career-high debut. But the real standout track from *Hit Me Hard and Soft* is "Birds of a Feather", a reflection on loyalty and connection, which now has over two billion streams on Spotify. It wasn't originally intended as a single but crept up the charts as it gained radio play, becoming #1 on the Hot Rock and Alternative Songs chart, #1 on the Pop Airplay chart, and eventually #2 on the Hot 100 to become one of Billie's biggest ever hits. Then "Wildflower" became a massive TikTok sensation, pushing the song back into the Top 40 towards the end of the year. Its parent album also enjoyed success well into the winter by remaining in the Billboard 200 Top 10 six months after its release.

The album was met with widespread critical acclaim, with many praising Billie's willingness to experiment while maintaining her signature sound.

Rolling Stone called it 'a bold, fearless record that cements Eilish as a generational talent', while *Pitchfork* noted that 'Eilish continues to innovate, delivering a sonically and emotionally complex project'.

NME gave the album a 5-star rating, calling it 'a masterclass in pushing boundaries while staying true to oneself ...there are upbeat bangers and a clear vision established for her artistry in the years to come... [it is] undeniably brighter in sound and more confident in its execution'.

Billie ended 2024 as Apple Music's Artist of the Year, in recognition of the impact of *Hit Me Hard and Soft.*

*Billie sang Birds of a Feather on Venice Beach, in her hometown of Los Angeles, in a performance beamed live to the Summer Olympics closing ceremony in Paris on 11 August 2024 as part of the handover to LA, which will host the Olympic Games in 2028.

Hit Me Hard and Soft

Release date: 17 May 2024
Record label: Darkroom/Interscope

Track list

Skinny
Lunch
Chihiro
Birds of a Feather *
Wildflower
The Greatest
L'Amour de Ma Vie
The Diner
Bittersuite
Blue

Set list

Chihiro
Lunch
NDA
Therefore I Am
Wildflower
When the Party's Over
The Diner
Ilomilo
Bad Guy
The Greatest
Male Fantasy
Skinny
TV
Bury a Friend
Oxytocin
You Should See Me in a Crown
Guess
Everything I Wanted
Blue
Lovely/Idontwannabeyouanymore/
Ocean Eyes
L'amour de Ma Vie/Over Now
What Was I Made For?
Happier Than Ever
Birds of a Feather

**from 29 September 2024 show in Quebec City*

The Hit Me Hard and Soft World Tour - September 2024-July 2025

To support the album, Billie set off on her spectacular *Hit Me Hard and Soft* World Tour in 2024, selling out arenas worldwide across North America, Oceania and Europe.

Featuring stunning visuals, immersive set designs, and a setlist taking in a selection of tracks from her trio of studio albums, the show won rave reviews. And that's despite the fact that, Billie was working without her brother Finneas, who was away touring his own solo album *For Cryin' Out Loud.* (Although Finneas did made a few surprise appearances in her New York run of shows.)

Her 'in the round' spectacular multimedia staging, featuring a digital performance floor, a floating platform, pyrotechnics and lasers, Billie succeeded in creating a vibe which one critic summed up perfectly as 'grandly intimate'.

Billboard's review of her sold-out shows in New York's Madison Square Garden said that her performance displayed her 'remarkable growth as a musician, vocalist, and performer, as well as her almost singular ability to cultivate intimacy in spaces that are diametrically opposed to that feeling.... and treated The Garden to some of the best and most adventurous pop music of the last half-decade'.

The *New York Times* said Billie brought 'a masterclass in intimacy to the arena stage' and praised her gift for 'dynamics, dramatics and audience engagement'.

Billie Eilish performs onstage during the Hit Me Hard and Soft Tour at The Kia Forum on December 21, 2024 in Inglewood, California.

The Hit Me Hard and Soft World Tour – September 2024-July 2025

September 2024

29	Videotron Center	Quebec City, Canada

October 2024

01/02	Scotiabank Arena	Toronto, Canada
04	CFG Bank Arena	Baltimore, USA
05	Wells Fargo Center	Philadelphia, USA
07	Little Caesars Arena	Detroit, USA
09	Prudential Center	Newark, USA
11	TD Garden	Boston, USA
13	PPG Paints Arena	Pittsburgh, USA
16-18	Madison Square Garden	NYC, USA

December 2024

03	Rogers Arena	Vancouver, Canada
05/06	Climate Pledge Arena	Seattle, USA
08	Moda Center	Portland, USA
10/11	SAP Center	San Jose, USA
13	Desert Diamond Arena	Glendale, USA
15-17	Kia Forum	Inglewood, USA
20/21	Kia Forum	Inglewood, USA

February 2025

18/19	Brisbane Entertainment Center	Brisbane, Australia
21/22	Brisbane Entertainment Center	Brisbane, Australia
24/25	Qudos Bank Arena	Sydney, Australia
27/28	Qudos Bank Arena	Sydney, Australia

March 2025

04/05	Rod Laver Arena	Melbourne, Australia
07/08	Rod Laver Arena	Melbourne, Australia
28/29	Royal Arena	Copenhagen, Denmark

● Billie Eilish performs onstage during Billie Eilish Hit Me Hard and Soft Tour Kick Off at Videotron Centre on September 29, 2024 in Quebec City, Quebec.

26

RODLAVER

April 2025

23/24	Avicii Arena	Stockholm. Sweden
26	Unity Arena	Baerum, Norway
28/29	Royal Arena	Copenhagen, Denmark

May 2025

02	ZAG-Arena	Hanover, Germany
04/05	Ziggo Dome	Amsterdam, Netherlands
07	Ziggo Dome	Amsterdam, Netherlands
09	Uber Arena	Berlin, Germany
29/30	Lanxess Arena	Cologne, Germany

June 2025

01	O2 Arena	Prague, Czech Republic
03/04	Tauron Arena	Krakow, Poland
06	Weiner Stadthalle	Vienna, Austria
08	Unipol Arena	Bologna, Italy
10/11	Accor Arena	Paris, France
14/15	Palau Sant Jordi	Barcelona, Spain

July 2025

07	OVO Hydro	Glasgow, Scotland
10/11	O2 Arena	London, UK
13/14	O2 Arena	London, UK
16/17	O2 Arena	London, UK
19/20	Co-op Live	Manchester, UK
22/23	Co-op Live	Manchester, UK
26	3 Arena	Dublin, Ireland

Billie Eilish performs her *Hit Me Hard and Soft Tour* at Rod Laver Arena on March 04, 2025 in Melbourne, Australia.

'Being an artist doesn't just mean you have a song. That doesn't make you an artist. The word 'artist' means so many different things, and I feel like to be a real one, you really have to do it all'.

Billie Eilish performs her *Hit Me Hard and Soft* Tour at Rod Laver Arena on March 04, 2025 in Melbourne, Australia.

All the good girls...

Although she is outspoken and uncompromising in interviews, and frequently heard swearing in the fly on the wall documentaries in which she features, her lyrics contain very little bad language. She doesn't take drugs or drink alcohol. As *Rolling Stone* magazine described her, she's 'an antihero who's safe to listen to with Mom and Dad in the car'.

Her Power

Conscious of the responsibility that comes with fame, Billie is thoughtful about her public pronouncements, because of the influence they will have on other young people. But that doesn't stop her speaking out about the causes that concern her.

Billie connects with fans by openly discussing the issues they all face around relationships, body image and mental health. In fact, she feels such a link with her audience that she won't even use the term 'fans', saying, 'I don't like that. They're literally just a part of my life; they're a part of my family. I don't think of them as on a lower level than me. I don't think I'm anything but equal to all of them. So yeah, they're basically all of my siblings'.

Having been brought up as a vegetarian, Billie is now vegan and an advocate for animal rights, having criticised the dairy, mink and wool industries for their practices.

She was recognised as Person of the Year by the animal rights organisation People for the Ethical Treatment of Animals organisation (PETA) in 2021.

Billie Eilish performs at Coachella Valley Music And Arts Festival on April 16, 2022 in Indio, California.

A dedicated advocate for sustainability, Billie continues her eco-conscious efforts by minimising waste and using renewable energy sources for her shows.

Once again Billie partnered with environmental nonprofit REVERB on her *Hit Me Hard and Soft World Tour* to reduce its ecological footprint. Sustainability efforts included reducing greenhouse gas pollution, decreasing single-use plastic waste, offering eco-friendly merchandise, and incorporating sustainable tour logistics. Fans attending her concerts are encouraged to participate in REVERB's "Music Climate Revolution" campaign, which helps offset carbon emissions and promotes environmental awareness. Billie is also a key figure and funder of REVERB's Music Decarbonisation Project, and, as part of this, also used solar powered stage lights.

During her international tour, Billie also champions various environmental organisations, and encourages fans to take a pledge to eat more plant-based foods.

Having regularly called out issues around body shaming, Billie has also recently discussed the damage and dangers around pornography, describing how she suffered nightmares after being exposed to 'abusive and violent' images from the age of just 11.

A good influence...

Billie was among the musicians added to the *Time* magazine annual list of the 100 most influential people in the world in September 2021. Her entry was written by Megan Thee Stallion who said; 'Billie Eilish is a unique soul, with a voice, style and attitude all unapologetically her own. She is a rare spirit who speaks from her heart with no pretences... a woman who stands up for herself and advocates for women everywhere'.

Billie Eilish performs during the virtual 2020 Democratic National Convention, August 20, 2020.

Billie Eilish accepts the Video for Good award for 'Your Power' onstage during the 2021 MTV Video Music Awards at Barclays Center on September 12, 2021 in the Brooklyn borough of New York City

She referenced the topic in her track "Male Fantasy" on *Happier Than Ever* and told interviewer Howard Stern that she now thinks porn 'is a disgrace' particularly for the way it can depict women's bodies and sexual experiences, skewering understanding of what is normal and what constitutes consent.

Billie said she believed viewing the content while so young had 'destroyed' her brain and caused her to suffer nightmares.

Venturing into the political arena, Billie encouraged her fans to register to vote in the 2020 US presidential election, endorsing the Democratic party and its candidate Joe Biden, as well as performing at the 2020 Democratic Convention. She and Finneas then endorsed the Kamala Harris-Tim Walz ticket in the 2024 US presidential election.

Awards

Billie has an impressive clutch of over 200 top awards to cementing her status as one of the most successful artists of the past 10 years, including ...

9 Grammy Awards (including sweeping the big four in 2020 with Album of the Year for *When We All Fall Asleep, Where Do We Go*? Record of the Year and Song of the Year for "Bad Guy" and Best New Artist) from 32 nominations

2 Academy Awards (Best Original Song for "No Time to Die" in 2022 and "What was I Made For?" in 2024)

2 Golden Globe Awards (2022 Best Original Song for "No Time to Die")

2 American Music Awards

19 Guinness World Records (including one for the most viewed Wikipedia page for a post-millennial with 39 million views, as verified on 5 May 2021)

7 MTV Video Music Awards and

4 Brit Awards (including International Artist of the Year 2022).

108.1 monthly million listeners on Spotify.

Finneas

Despite his stellar success as a songwriter and producer for various artists, there is no doubt that Finneas' most stunning achievement is masterminding Billie's ascent from his bedroom to the world stage as one of the music industry's brightest stars. Considering his and Billie's achievements he said, 'I think we have benefitted from being the odd one out. When you hear a truly generic pop song – and I don't use that word with negative connotations, just in the sense of standard – by the time you get to the second verse, you know exactly what the rest of the song sounds like.

'I think where a song doesn't go is as interesting as where a song goes. Sometimes we'll put in a different chorus, just for the slap in the face of, like, "Your brain has to stay awake for this"'.

As well as producing and co-writing for Billie, Finneas also makes his own music and has solo-headlined shows, including his 2025 *For Cryin' Out Loud* tour, visiting 11 countries including Australia, New Zealand and a run of UK and European dates.

He released a solo single, "New Girl", in 2016, and a debut EP called *Blood Harmony* in 2019. His debut studio album, *Optimist*, was released in October 2021 and his second album *For Cryin' Out Loud*! arrived in October 2024.

He balances his solo ventures by building up an impressive CV including projects with high-profile artists, Drake, Nicki Minaj, Selena Gomez, Camila Cabello, Demi Lovato, Halsey and Kid Cudi, among many others.

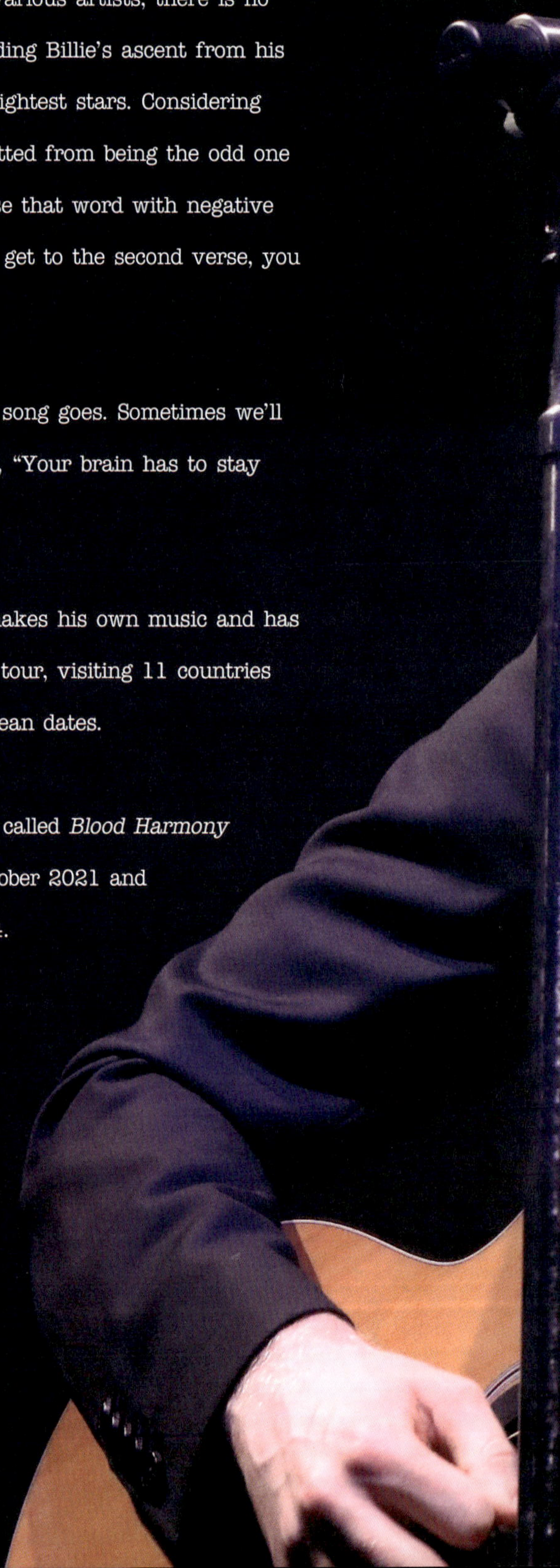

Finneas performs at The Danforth Music Hall on November 21, 2021 in Toronto, Ontario.

Taylor

Billie Eilish performs during the Austin City Limits (ACL) Music festival at Zilker Park on October 9, 2021 in Austin, Texas.

Billie

Through all the crazy times since she catapulted to global fame, Billie has always kept it real. Her family are massively important in keeping her grounded and she frequently talks about how lucky she is to have them in her life, helping her to navigate the madness that comes with 21st century celebrity.

One of the biggest stars on the planet by any measure, her achievements include clocking up over 45 billion total streams for her music worldwide. Her YouTube channel had 54.7 million subscribers and attracted 18 billion views across her 144 uploads as of February 2025.

This phenomenal success comes in spite of her refusal to conform to industry ideals of female artists, preferring instead to stick to her often grim, anxiety-laden subject matter and shocking delivery with her body swaddled in oversized clothing to remove it from the equation.

Although she has frequently commented that she does not want to be any kind of role model, it seems to be happening anyway as she discusses her mental health issues and her recently announced queer identity.

Billie first 'came out' in a November 2023 cover story with "Variety", telling the magazine, 'I've never really felt like I could relate to girls very well. I love them so much. I love them as people. I'm attracted to them as people. I'm attracted to them for real ...I'm physically attracted to them. But I'm also so intimidated by them and their beauty and their presence'.

Seemingly surprised both by her own public words and the reaction to the news, she said a few weeks later, 'I didn't [know I was coming out], but I kinda thought, wasn't it obvious?' she said. 'I didn't realise people didn't know'.

'I saw the article, and I was like, "Oh, I guess I came out today!" I just don't really believe in [coming out]. I'm just like, why can't we just exist? I've been doing this for a long time, and I just didn't talk about it.

'It's exciting to me because I guess people didn't know, so it's cool that they know...I am for the girls'.

She underlined her interest in all things female in August 2024 when she collaborated with British star Charli xcx for a remix of Charli's track "Guess", all about guessing the colour of a girl's underwear. The track, originally from the deluxe version of Charli's hit album *Brat*, was a huge hit when remixed with Billie's verses, scooping the 2025 Brit Award for Song of the Year as well as topping the charts in the UK and making #12 on the Billboard Hot 100.

'I think it's really cool when artists have song titles or album names that are a really conversational sentence'.

Billie Eilish, Charli XCX at the Billie Eilish *Hit Me Hard and Soft Tour* at Kia Forum on December 17, 2024 in Inglewood, California.

The accompanying video, including shots of Billie and Charli walking as underwear falls on them like rain from the sky, was filmed just four days before the track was released and when she accepted her Brit Award, Charli thanked Billie for her involvement and for 'moving with pace', adding that, 'not all artists are spontaneous, despite them claiming that they are, so thank you Billie for running and gunning with me which was very cool'.

Having clearly broken the mould for her generation, Billie's ability to speak to the Gen-Z population and help them feel accepted in society seems sure to continue as she grows older.

It's exciting to wonder what she'll do next...